FROM CONFRONTATION TO NEGOTIATION

U.S. Relations with Cuba

About the Book and Author

Nearly thirty years have passed since the United States first attempted to overthrow the fledgling Castro government. Despite enormous changes in the hemisphere, significant developments in the nature of Cuba's international relations, and an end to the cold war consensus in the United States that quietly sanctioned interference in and obstruction of Third World politics, U.S. policy toward Cuba has changed very little: It still embodies the failed dream of isolating Cuba and destroying the Cuban revolution.

In *From Confrontation to Negotiation: U.S. Relations with Cuba,* Philip Brenner provides a thoughtful overview of U.S.-Cuban relations since 1898, with an emphasis on the past ten years. Assumptions, goals, and continuities in U.S. policy are highlighted. He then offers a clear picture of the issues that divide the two countries and around which any discussions for a normalization of relations would likely turn.

Could discussions occur? Is a call for a less hostile relationship between the United States and Cuba politically feasible? What are the chances that Cuba and the United States can actually work out an accommodation? Dr. Brenner analyzes the domestic political factors in each country that shape policy and that might present possibilities for serious discussion. He then proposes a workable alternative Cuban policy for the United States that takes into account the fundamental concerns of both countries. The policy proposal is related to the framework adopted by Policy Alternatives for the Caribbean and Central America (PACCA).

Philip Brenner is associate professor of international relations at The American University, where he teaches in the Washington Semester Program. He is a member of the board of the National Security Archive and is author of *The Limits and Possibilities of Congress* (1983).

FROM CONFRONTATION TO NEGOTIATION

U.S. Relations with Cuba

Philip Brenner

A PACCA BOOK

WESTVIEW PRESS
BOULDER AND LONDON

Copyright © 1988 by Policy Alternatives for the Caribbean and Central America

Published in 1988 in the United States of America by Westview Press, Inc.; Frederick A. Praeger, Publisher; 5500 Central Avenue, Boulder, Colorado 80301

Library of Congress Cataloging-in-Publication Data
Brenner, Philip.
  From confrontation to negotiation: U.S. relations with Cuba/
Philip Brenner.
    p. cm.
  Bibliography: p.
  Includes index.
  ISBN 0-8133-7507-X. ISBN 0-8133-7509-6 (pbk.)
  1. United States—Foreign relations—Cuba. 2. Cuba—Foreign
relations—United States. 3. United States—Foreign
relations—1981–   4. Cuba—Foreign relations—1959–   I. Title.
E183.8.C9B74 1988
327.7307291—dc19   87-33985
                                                    CIP

Printed and bound in the United States of America

The paper used in this publication meets the requirements of the American National Standard for Permanence of Paper for Printed Library Materials Z39.48-1984.

10   9   8   7   6   5   4   3   2   1

Contents

Acknowledgments

THIS BOOK EVOLVED from a short paper prepared for a conference sponsored by Policy Alternatives for the Caribbean and Central America (PACCA), an association of scholars and policymakers. Its development owes much to the dedicated effort of the people associated with PACCA—as well as to those not affiliated with the organization—who gave much time helping me to refine the analysis and to elaborate essential portions of the book. In this sense the book was a group project, though its flaws remain mine.

A few people provided extensive comments on the entire manuscript (and in some instances on several drafts of the manuscript). Much appreciation goes to Sylvia Arrom, Carolee Bengelsdorf, Carmen Diana Deere, Saul Landau, and William LeoGrande. Several others gave me very useful suggestions at various stages in the project and no doubt will recognize their handiwork in the final product: Michael Conroy, Margaret Crahan, Xabier Gorostiaga, Richard Fagen, Peter Hakim, Rafael Hernandez, Stuart Lippe, Charles William Maynes, Marifeli Perez-Stable, Robert Pastor, Barry Sklar, Wayne Smith, and Raul Suarez.

Essential to the entire project have been the untiring efforts of the PACCA staff—Robert Stark, Colin Danby, and Alicia Torres. They helped to make this a group project by coordinating the disparate network of scholars who contributed to the creation of the book. Their concern about the book's audience, manifested through consultations with key people and through follow-up and study guides, will help make the book more useful to students, scholars, and policymakers.

My editors at Westview Press—Barbara Ellington, Beverly LeSuer, and Marian Safran—asked insightful questions that sharpened the analysis and suggested changes that in every instance enhanced the quality of the book. It was a pleasure to work with professionals who pay such scrupulous attention to detail.

I received significant support from The American University, which provided a research grant that enabled me to compile data for the book and to write one draft. Additional assistance came from the National Security Archive, the National Council on United States–Cuban Relations, and PACCA for trips to Cuba during which I conducted interviews with Cuban leaders.

Some authors are lucky enough to have parents who take a small interest in their work. I had the great fortune that my mother, Lillian Brenner, also provided essential research for the book. With great love, devotion, and intelligence, she would scour newspapers and magazines for articles about Cuba and rush them to me.

My daughter, Sarah, was born during the course of writing this book. The unending joy she brings bolstered me on dreary days and added special purpose to the project. My hope is that the book can contribute to reduced tension between the United States and Cuba and thereby help to promote a more peaceful world for her.

Throughout the creation of this book, from its days as a brief essay to its development as papers presented at scholarly meetings to its unfolding through several drafts, my wife, Betsy Vieth, has given me wise counsel, enthusiastic support, and a home atmosphere conducive to inquiry and writing. Ultimately the book was a family project too.

Philip Brenner

Introduction:
———— Realism About Cuba

AT A MEETING OF THE JOINT CHIEFS OF STAFF a few months before the U.S.-sponsored Bay of Pigs invasion in April 1961, talk among the generals began to turn casually around the possibility of an invasion by U.S. troops. To the commandant of the Marine Corps, General David M. Shoup, it was clear that his colleagues envisioned Cuba as a small island, perhaps a hundred miles long. He realized that an invasion plan based on such a major misperception would lead to nothing less than catastrophe, and in horror he superimposed a map of Cuba over one of the United States. The "small island" stretched from New York to Chicago.[1]

That was neither the first time, nor the last, that U.S. officials had tried to come up with an easy solution for dealing with Cuba, based on misperceptions about it. For 150 years, would-be U.S. statesmen have seen Cuba variously as a sleepy island that could be bought, annexed, or crushed; as a mindless, unsure neophyte waiting to be wooed; and today as a puppet of the Soviet Union that threatens fundamental U.S. security. Yet Cuba does not lend itself to such facile characterizations that provide ready policy prescriptions.

Instead U.S. policy should be developed on the basis of the Cuban reality, which is complex:

- Cuba is only ninety miles from the United States, and this proximity offers the potential for economic, political, and social interaction; but Cuba also has a special relationship with the

1

Soviet Union, which does pose a potential threat to the United States;

- Its relationship with the Soviet Union provides significant security for Cuba; but it also makes Cuba uncomfortably vulnerable as a strategic target of the United States;
- U.S. dominance over Cuba before 1959 has left many marks on Cuba's culture: Baseball is the national sport, and symbols of the United States, such as jeans and rock music, are popular today; but the earlier relationship of subservience makes Cuba wary of the United States;
- One important link between the two countries is the more than one million Cuban-Americans in the United States who have emigrated since the 1959 revolution that brought Fidel Castro to power; but most are hostile to the regime in Cuba;
- Cuba is smaller than most countries in Latin America, though its population of 10.1 million people and land area of 43,000 square miles is greater than any country in Central America or the Caribbean; but it has the kind of influence with many Third World countries that is more typical of a larger nation.

This complexity does not make a viable policy unattainable. It only means that the policy must be rooted in a clear picture of Cuba and be responsive to real U.S. interests. A stark, undifferentiated image of a Cuban threat distorts reality and leads the United States to take actions against its own interest.

Cuba is one of the few countries in the world with which the United States does not have normal relations. Yet the United States cannot ignore Cuba. Not only is Cuba too close geographically, but it is also an important country in the region and has significant influence in the Third World. The question for the United States is not *whether* it will relate to Cuba. The question is *how* it will relate to Cuba.

The choices are either confrontation or negotiation. Since 1960 the United States has opted for the former. There is little benefit in this approach, and confrontation with Cuba generates tension that ripples throughout the hemisphere and needlessly increases the danger of a major conflict between the superpowers. Negotiation, in contrast, holds out the potential for the United States to secure several interests. Indeed, both countries would benefit from a rapprochement.

To be sure, the road from confrontation to negotiation would be more like an obstacle course than a freeway. It is littered with U.S. fears about Cuban communism and with Cuba's concerns about its own security and development. It is darkened by the history of U.S. domination over the island, by the Cuban missile crisis, and by the distrust built up between the two countries since 1959.

Thus, the process of rapprochement between the United States and Cuba will entail a sensitive reconciliation of U.S. interests and Cuban concerns. This book focuses on these interests and concerns. It examines the history of the relationship between the two countries during the twentieth century, highlights their difference today, and explores how the politics in each country might enable the United States and Cuba to pursue a reconciliation. The concluding chapter outlines an alternative U.S. policy toward Cuba that could enhance U.S. interests, alleviate Cuban concerns, and move the two countries from confrontation to negotiation.

Notes

1. David Halberstam, *The Best and the Brightest* (Greenwich, Conn.: Fawcett, 1973), pp. 84–85.

CHAPTER 1

U.S. Policy Toward Cuba, 1898–1980

"THE UNITED STATES NEVER REMEMBERS and Latin America never forgets" is a well-known Latin American aphorism that succinctly explains the depth of Cuban distrust of the United States and the continuing surprise North Americans manifest about Cuban behavior. Cuban national pride is fierce, and for the better part of a hundred years the United States undermined, disparaged, and ignored Cuban sovereignty. To be sure, the United States acted toward much of Latin America with an arrogance that Abraham Lowenthal has characterized aptly as a "hegemonic presumption."[1] Cuba experienced the full brunt of the treatment because in many ways it was the jewel in the U.S. imperial crown (the "pearl of the Antilles") for the first half of the twentieth century.

Between 1898 and 1934, the United States robbed Cuba of the sovereignty it had fought hard to win from Spain. The United States controlled Cuba's politics and dominated its economy. Then from 1934 to 1958 Cuba was a favored locale for U.S. investors and tourists, and the two countries maintained a special relationship that worked largely to the benefit of the United States. This relationship was destroyed by the 1959 revolution.

The greater part of this chapter will focus on the period after 1959. The sweep of events before 1959 will be subsumed in the first section, and the period between the revolution and the Ronald Reagan administration will be divided into two segments, 1959–1970 and 1971–1980. Current U.S. policy will be examined in Chapter 2.

From Independence War to Revolution

What North Americans commonly refer to as the 1898 Spanish-American War—when the United States fought against Spain for three months in Cuba and in the Philippines—is to the Cubans and Filipinos an episode in their respective wars of independence against Spain. The seemingly insignificant difference in name reflects a deeper tendency in the United States over the last century to see Cuba and Cuban events as an extension of the United States and U.S. interests. Cuba was a colony of Spain until 1898. But even before independence, the United States had begun to replace Spain as the dominant force in Cuban economic affairs.

By the time Cubans began a concerted struggle for independence from Spain in 1868, Spanish dominance over Cuban trade already had declined. In 1860, Cuba sent 62 percent of its exports to the United States and only 3 percent to Spain. Then, between 1868 and 1878, the war for independence wreaked havoc on the midsized sugar farms predominant in Cuban agriculture until then. With the surviving smaller farms becoming easy prey for investors, most were combined into large units linked to a central mill. One U.S. company, Havemeyer's American Sugar Refining Company, owned nineteen of these *centrales* (mills) and supplied more than 70 percent of the sugar consumed in the United States. Increasingly, American Sugar came to rely on Cuba as its source for cane.[2]

Beginning with the sugar connection, Cuban dependence on its wealthy neighbor grew rapidly by the turn of the century. Though U.S. investment in Cuba had reached no more than an estimated $50 million in 1896, much of it was in key sectors. By 1902, U.S. corporations had invested $100 million, and U.S. banks had begun to influence Cuba's finances by way of loans.[3]

At various times in the nineteenth century, the idea of annexing Cuba was raised in the United States. But this idea was dashed before the Civil War by opposition from northern states, which feared the admission of another slave state to the union, and after 1865 by those who objected to the preponderance of nonwhites on the island. In 1898, when the United States intervened in the independence war, economic interests were an important motivating force for the action.

The Cubans had nearly won the war by February, when the U.S. battleship *Maine*—in Havana harbor to protect U.S. property and to signal to the Cuban rebels that the United States was worried about the course the revolution would take—exploded. Fueled by sensational articles in Hearst's *New York Journal,* a war frenzy developed in the United States. In April, the United States declared war against Spain, and in June, 17,000 U.S. troops joined in the Cuban struggle for independence. They fought against a weary and weakened Spanish force, which surrendered quickly at the end of July.[4] The United States claimed credit for the victory over Spain and promptly installed a military government to oversee affairs. Historian Jules Benjamin has explained that U.S. military occupation contributed to the transformation of Cuba from the status of Spanish colony to that of a U.S. quasi-colony: "The Military Government under General Leonard Wood fostered the development of the island by U.S. capital. . . . General Wood, like most U.S. policymakers after him, saw stability in Cuba arising from her ability and willingness to obtain U.S. capital."[5]

Wood was a strong advocate of tariff reciprocity, which "he saw as a step toward the annexation" of Cuba.[6] Tariff reciprocity, ultimately approved by the U.S. Congress in 1903, tied Cuba to U.S. corporations and undermined indigenous Cuban enterprises. Under the 1903 agreement, U.S. goods became less expensive in Cuba than those from any other country—cheaper even than those produced in Cuba. In addition, as economist Louis Perez explained: "Preferential access to U.S. markets for Cuban agricultural products at once encouraged Cuban dependency on sugar and tobacco and increased foreign control over these vital sectors of the economy. Reciprocity also discouraged economic diversification by promoting the consolidation of land from small units into the latifundia [large plantations] and concentration of ownership from local family to foreign corporation."[7]

If economic dependence on the United States firmly closed the lid over the coffin of Cuban independence, the lid's hinges were attached in 1901. That year, the United States forced Cuba to include the Platt Amendment in its new constitution, as a condition for the removal of the occupying U.S. force. Introduced by Senator Orville Platt and approved by the U.S. Congress as part of an army appropriations bill, the amendment limited Cuban sovereignty by stipulating that the United States could intervene in all Cuban affairs, domestic or foreign, solely at U.S. discretion. This meant that the United States was free to send in troops as if Cuba were a colony and in effect, to dictate to Cubans how they could organize their government and society.[8] The Platt Amendment also required Cuba to sell or lease to the United States land for a naval base, which still exists today as Guantanamo Naval Base.

Under these broad terms, the United States did send troops to Cuba three times in the next thirty-two years to stabilize situations that threatened U.S. property. One of these interventions lasted for a period of three years (1906–1909), during which time U.S. troops served again as an occupation force with a military governor. More importantly, the threat of intervention gave the United States de facto control over the internal affairs of the country. Cuban politicians understood that they had to seek U.S. approval to select a president. The State Department made clear that the Cuban government had to facilitate the penetration of the Cuban economy by U.S. corporations and had to avoid placing undue restrictions (such as taxes) on these enterprises.[9] U.S. officials stated publicly that they sought to bring democracy and morality to Cuban affairs, and some of them may have been imbued with a Wilsonian idealism that sought to make the world safe for democracy. But under U.S. auspices, Cuban governments were corrupt and elections were generally rigged.

Circumstances also contributed to the loss of Cuba's sovereignty to the United States. As a result of the 1920–1921 depression in the sugar industry, U.S. banks and sugar companies gained an ever greater foothold on the economy through consolidation. Their investment in Cuba totaled over $600 million—1,100 percent greater than it had been in 1898. U.S.-owned mills produced 60 percent of Cuba's sugar, and U.S. companies controlled 90 percent of Cuba's electrical generating capacity.[10] Direct private U.S. investment in Cuba totaled $1 billion in 1927.[11]

Dependency meant that Cuba could not invest in potential farm land for food production. The result was that nearly one-third of Cuba's food had to be imported, including items such as vegetables that could have been grown domestically. Dependency also meant that Cuba could not provide for basic needs that were unrelated to the productive capacity for sugar and could not sustain independent development. Its needs were serviced by imports. This deepened its dependence on the United States, from which it purchased 80 percent of these foreign goods and services.[12] Louis Perez described how dependency robbed Cuba of nationhood and made it into a quasi-colony of the United States: Once U.S. corporations began to invest heavily in Cuba in the late 1800s, Cuban planters functioned "as agents of North American capital, instruments of U.S. economic penetration of Cuba, and advocates of U.S. intervention. . . . A new habit developed in Cuba, a practice to endure into the twentieth century, in which the local bourgeoisie [capitalists], able to petition the United States in its behalf in its disputes with local authority, looked to Washington for the defense of privilege and property."[13]

The Cuban government itself was tied closely to U.S. banks because the banks lent it large sums for public works projects. As the 1929 depression hit Cuba especially hard, there were few resources with which to repay the loans. By 1932 the government was bankrupt, and the foreign debt was over $100 million. Concern over the banks' solvency gave the United States added impetus to intervene in Cuban affairs.[14]

One of President Franklin Roosevelt's important foreign policy initiatives in 1933 was the Good Neighbor Policy. The newly elected Democratic president offered it as a contrast to the "gunboat diplomacy" that the Republicans had practiced in Latin America. Under the Good Neighbor Policy, the United States would supposedly eschew military intervention and attempt to relate to countries in the hemisphere by appeals to common interests as "neighbors." Still, the Roosevelt administration had no compunction about trying to control Cuban affairs. In the summer of 1933, Assistant Secretary of State Sumner Welles assumed the mantle ambassador plenipotentiary to Cuba and in the next year orchestrated key events to serve the U.S. business interests.[15]

At the time, Cuba was ruled by the dictatorial government of Gerardo Machado. By the early 1930s, his brutality had led to such instability that the United States began to distance itself from the dictator and then encouraged him to step down.[16] Ambassador Welles supported the rising tide of anti-Machado opponents and helped to select and organize the government that emerged out of the successful August 1933 coup. When a September revolt ousted the Welles-backed officials, the ambassador immediately applied pressure. He advocated armed intervention, encouraged nonrecognition of the new government, and began to work with the army to plan the overthrow of the new government. By January 1934 his plans had worked to wreck the September revolution, and a government friendly to U.S. economic interests was installed. Welles then helped to fashion plans for the Cuban economy.[17]

While the Roosevelt administration was restructuring the Cuban debt, it facilitated the further penetration of U.S. capital and tied Cuba even more closely to the United States through a series of trade agreements. Even though in the next twenty-five years U.S. businesses lost some ground to other foreign investors and some Cuban nationals gained a small foothold, by 1958 U.S. companies had made Cuba their second largest investment location in Latin America. Cuba sent 71 percent of its exports to the United States in 1958, and 64 percent of Cuba's imports came from there.[18] Treaties of 1934 formally negated the right of the United States to intervene under the Platt Amendment, but economic power enabled the United States to continue its major role in Cuban affairs.[19]

From 1934 to 1958, Cuban leaders regularly consulted with U.S. officials and staunchly followed U.S. foreign policy directions.[20] In this period the United States was less inclined than it had been in the first third of the century to specify the particular Cuban politicians it wanted to govern Cuba. But it did make clear the contours of acceptable behavior within which Cuba had to conduct itself. Of greatest importance, Cuba had to maintain economic and political stability, which meant that the state had to respect and protect property relations, suppress labor struggles, and keep Cuba open to foreign capital.[21]

Toward this end, the Cuban military played a significant role in defining the political order. Its most significant figure was Fulgencio Batista, who led the effort to overthrow the interim government in 1933 after the Machado downfall and who was elected president in 1940 for a four-year term. Batista and the army made clear that they were ardent followers of the U.S. guidelines, in contrast to the suspect inclinations of other Cuban leaders at the time who had been nurtured by the nationalism of the early 1930s. Thus, the United States readily recognized the dictatorship Batista created in 1952, when he seized power shortly before the scheduled presidential election of that year.[22]

In the next six years, the corruption that had been characteristic of Cuban politics throughout the century reached new heights. This corruption, combined with government brutality, generated a widespread opposition to the dictatorship among all classes in the country. The opposition took the form in the cities of an underground movement, which coordinated efforts with guerrilla groups in the rural areas. The most prominent of the latter was the July 26th Movement, headed by Fidel Castro Ruz.[23] Castro had captured popular imagination in the United States following a series of on-the-scenes stories from the Sierra Maestra by *New York Times* reporter Herbert Matthews in February 1957.[24] Castro was described as an idealistic fighter, from a middle-class background, who hoped to bring social reforms and democracy to Cuba.

As Batista responded with increased violence to the growing opposition and to his loss of legitimacy, there was a common view in the U.S. government that the United States had to end its ties to the dictator, encourage him to step down, and find a nonrevolutionary solution to the turmoil that could safeguard U.S. investments.[25] Early in 1958, the United States withdrew one of the remaining girders from Batista's tottering regime. It embargoed new orders for the military equipment and ammunition that had provided the wherewithal for Batista's repression. However, it did allow the continued delivery of weaponry that had been previously contracted. This ambivalent action reflected disagreements among the U.S. ambassador, the Central Intelligence Agency (CIA), and the State Department about how to deal with Batista and with the growing instability. In retrospect, there was little the United States could have done, short of an invasion, to alter the course of events that year. Batista maintained his position until New Year's Eve 1958, when he fled the country, and on January 8, 1959, Fidel Castro marched triumphantly into Havana.

From Conflict to Cold War: 1959–1970

There continues to be a debate about whether the United States "pushed" Cuba into the arms of the Soviet Union, or whether the revolutionary leadership had long been committed to Marxism-Leninism. (The debate has taken on particular poignance now, as some analysts see the history of relations with Cuba as a harbinger of relations with Nicaragua.) The simple answer is that because Cuban history did not begin in 1959, both sides of the debate have validity.[26]

The revolutionaries inherited lessons from earlier, failed efforts at reform. As in 1933, the failures often were due in part to U.S. machinations, and thus the United States was viewed with suspicion. The Cuban leaders had great skepticism about Soviet intentions, too, in part because of their hostility toward the Moscow-oriented Communist parties of Latin America. But they shared a Marxist-Leninist language with communists.

Among U.S. officials, this was sufficient evidence to condemn the fidelistas. U.S. leaders inherited an outlook that conditioned them to view revolutionaries with skepticism in the first place and to see communism as a seamless, international conspiracy. In the period from 1959 to 1970, the weight of history left its imprint on the agendas of the Cuban revolutionaries and U.S. officials and helped to shape the ensuing conflict between the United States and Cuba.

There is little doubt that the July 26th Movement was committed to major social and economic changes in Cuba. In a 1957 manifesto the movement declared agrarian reform and the redistribution of income to be major goals; it promised to end illiteracy, improve health care, and modernize rural areas. Yet specific ways of implementing these goals had not been articulated when the revolution occurred. Even before a working policy had been hammered out by the revolutionary government in 1959, the Cuban upper class initiated counterrevolutionary actions, such as sabotage, against the new government.

In Washington, the Dwight Eisenhower administration watched the unfolding revolution without a clear determination about what course the United States would follow. Tad Szulc reported that as early as March 10, 1959—at a point when "the Cubans had not yet seized or nationalized any American property"—the National Security Council (NSC) included on its agenda "as a principal topic the modalities of bringing 'another government to power in Cuba.' "[27] Yet it appears that the NSC did not decide on a particular modality then. There were still voices in the administration, such as that of Ambassador Philip Bonsal, that argued in favor of U.S. restraint and caution. In their view, the direction in which the revolution itself or Cuban foreign policy would go was not yet determined.[28]

By mid-1959, however, proponents of accommodation within the administration had been routed, and the administration clearly had opted for some form of antagonistic relationship. This was evident in meetings with Cuban diplomats, in negotiations over sugar, and in the arms provided to the counterrevolutionaries. When Fidel Castro traveled to Washington in April 1959, seeking to establish some modus vivendi with the United States, President Eisenhower made a point of going golfing in Georgia during the visit.[29]

From the outset, officials in the new Cuban government feared U.S. intervention. The history of U.S. marines in Cuba was seared in the mind-set of every Cuban patriot, and these officials were particularly sensitive to the U.S. overthrow of the Jacobo Arbenz government in Guatemala only five years earlier. In that case, the United States had been motivated by three factors: the nationalization of unused fertile land, much of which belonged to the United Fruit Company; the import of weapons from Czechoslovakia and what appeared to be the development of a relationship with the Soviet bloc; and extensive social reforms within Guatemala. In order to avoid a similar provocation of the United States, the Cubans at first did not nationalize the holdings of large sugar companies.[30] In addition, initially they stayed quite a distance from the Soviet Union, which had shown little interest in the Cuban revolution. It was not until February 1960 that a high-level Soviet delegation traveled to the island.[31]

By this time U.S. public opinion had begun to shift against the new Cuban government because of the "show" trials of former Batista soldiers and press reports that Cuba had the likelihood of becoming socialist. In mid-1960, Secretary of State Christian Herter demanded that the three U.S. oil companies in Cuba refuse to refine a pending shipment of crude from the Soviet Union. Castro retaliated by nationalizing the refineries, and soon thereafter the United States stopped the importation of Cuban sugar by reducing Cuba's sugar quota to zero. Then, on January 3, 1961, in one of his last major acts in office, President Eisenhower broke diplomatic relations with Cuba.

Ten months earlier the U.S. president had authorized preparation of an invasion of the island by 1,500 Cuban exiles, who were trained and supplied by the CIA. The invasion became the ill-fated Bay of Pigs episode of April 17–19, 1961 (early in John F. Kennedy's presidency).[32] It was on April 16, at the public funeral for those who died in the preinvasion bombing of Havana airport, that Castro first declared Cuba to be a "socialist" country.[33]

Upon reflection, President Kennedy might have been remorseful and chastened because the invasion flagrantly violated international law. Instead, he authorized expenditures for a prolonged covert war against Cuba and established the overthrow of the Cuban government as a firm foreign policy goal of his administration. The covert war involved at least ten attempts to assassinate Fidel Castro; weekly landings in Cuba of arms, supplies, and mercenary soldiers for antigovernment forces fighting largely in the Escambray Mountains; the illegal creation and maintenance of a large CIA base in Florida to support the war; and sabotage of Cuban agriculture and industry. The sabotage included the destruction of machinery, the burning of fields, and the poisoning of harvested crops bound for export.[34]

Cuba was no longer exporting anything to the United States. Though the formal economic embargo was instituted on February 6, 1962, nearly all trade with Cuba had ended shortly after the United States had set the Cuban sugar quota at zero, in December 1960. To a country whose economy had been tied to the United States, these actions were an attempt at strangulation. Cuba could sell sugar, cigars, and nickel elsewhere (though finding new buyers quickly was a problem), but the replacement parts for its U.S.-made machinery, its trucks, and its hospital equipment had to come from the United States. It needed to buy goods internationally on credit with an acceptable hard currency, but U.S. banks forced international lending agencies and the financial institutions of other Western countries to cut off Cuba's credit. In 1964 the United States persuaded the Organization of American States (OAS) to institute a hemispheric embargo against Cuba.[35]

Thus the Eisenhower, Kennedy, and Lyndon Johnson administrations in short order firmly planted the first two roots of U.S. policy toward revolutionary Cuba: overthrow the Cuban government and isolate it. Isolation was intended partly to cripple and topple the government and partly to contain Cuba's influence on other countries where social and economic conditions made them candidates for revolution.

This policy toward Cuba emanated from several sources. First, the prior relationship with Cuba, in which the United States had dominated Cuban politics, led Washington officials to resent and distrust a government they could not control. Officials also saw the revolution from the perspective of corporations, which bemoaned the loss of a treasure from which they had reaped great profits. Companies that suffered losses in Cuba due to expropriations pressured the U.S. government to redress their damages. Some officials feared domestic political reprisal. They remembered the purges in the State Department ten years earlier, after the United States "lost" China, and the way in which unscrupulous politicians in the 1950s had attacked elected officials who were not dogmatically anticommunist. Indeed, the rigid anticommunist ideological framework that dominated the U.S. foreign policy debate ultimately shaped policy toward Cuba. It forced policymakers to misconstrue an indigenous revolution as a marker in the East-West struggle.[36]

The Congress, too, encouraged a hostile posture toward Cuba in speeches and in a series of laws intended to facilitate the policy. It amended the 1961 Foreign Assistance Act, the 1917 Trading with the Enemy Act, and the 1949 Export Administration Act to give the president authority to ban all trade and financial transactions with Cuba. In 1962 the House and Senate passed a joint resolution that declared: "The United States is determined to prevent by whatever means may be necessary, including the use of arms, the Marxist-Leninist regime in Cuba from extending, by force or the threat of force, its aggressive or subversive activities to any part of this hemisphere; . . . and to work with the Organization of American States and with freedom-loving Cubans to support the aspirations of the Cuban people for self-determination" (Public Law 87-733).

It would have been difficult to sustain the credibility of the claim that Cuba alone was a real threat to U.S. security. Moreover, other Latin American nations were loathe to endorse U.S. intervention against any country in the region because of their own sorry experience with the hovering giant. What made the Cuban threat credible and assuaged the Latin Americans was the specter of "International Communism." Cuba had turned to the Soviet Union, China, and other socialist countries for assistance when the United States cut off trade and aid. The cold war was still very much alive in the early 1960s, and one of its tenets was that communist countries formed a monolithic bloc. Cuba was now seen as a member of the bloc. When the Organization of American States voted to suspend Cuba's membership in January 1962, it resolved that "the present connections of the Government of Cuba with the Sino-Soviet bloc of countries are evidently incompatible with the principles and standards that govern the regional system."[37] The revelation, in October 1962, that the Soviet Union had placed missiles in Cuba legitimated warnings about the communist threat less than one hundred miles from Florida. The missile crisis brought the two superpowers the closest they had ever been to nuclear war, and Cuba was in the center of the conflict.

On October 14 a U-2 reconnaissance flight over Cuba confirmed reports that the Soviet Union was building facilities for intermediate range ballistic missiles (IRBMs) at several locations. On October 22, President Kennedy announced that the United States had initiated a naval blockade to prevent completion of the missile sites, and he demanded the facilities be dismantled. Tension mounted as Soviet ships steamed toward Cuba and waiting U.S. warships, and the United States placed its strategic forces on the highest level of alert they have ever been placed.

For thirteen days the ExCom, a small group of advisers close to President Kennedy, debated over strategies to resolve the crisis, including air strikes against the missiles. On October 27 a U-2 reconnaissance plane was shot down over Cuba. It is still unclear today whether it was destroyed by a surface-to-air missile (SAM) fired by the Soviets, whether Cubans got control of a SAM missile and used it, or whether the Cubans shot down the U-2 with antiaircraft weapons they controlled. Later that day, Attorney General Robert F. Kennedy delivered an ultimatum to Soviet Ambassador Anatoly Dobrynin. It threatened that the United States would use air strikes against the missiles if they were not removed within forty-eight hours, or would strike immediately if another U-2 were downed. Twelve hours later Soviet Premier Nikita Khrushchev ordered the IRBMs dismantled. In return, President Kennedy explicitly promised that the United States would not invade Cuba, and he indicated, though did not explicitly promise, that the United States would remove missiles from Turkey.[38]

It appears that the missiles in Turkey played an important role in prompting the Soviets to place missiles in Cuba. Turkey is as close to the Soviet Union as Cuba is to the United States, and Soviet leaders perceived that the United States was preparing a first strike against the Soviet Union. In fact, in 1962 the United States had overwhelming nuclear superiority over the Soviet Union, the Soviet

Union did not have a credible deterrent against a first strike, and a first strike was one of the five approved U.S. nuclear war operational plans. The forty IRBMs the Soviet Union was sending to Cuba would not have given it a first-strike capacity against the United States. But the missiles did hold out the credible potential to counter a first strike with an unacceptably damaging second strike.

Cuba was motivated to request the missiles because it had believed the United States was preparing for another invasion and the U.S. covert war itself was taking a mounting toll. Cuba sought a way to raise the costs of U.S. intervention, by creating a trip-wire deterrent. With Soviet missiles on the island, a U.S. invasion would necessarily involve the Soviet Union, potentially escalating a U.S.-Cuban conflict into a superpower confrontation. Cuba hoped this potential would deter the United States from attempting an invasion. Yet Cuban leaders were not pleased with the outcome of the crisis whereby the United States pledged not to invade Cuba in return for the removal of Soviet missiles. They were angered that the Soviets had reached the agreement without consulting them.[39]

In the next six years Cuba expressed its displeasure with the Soviet Union in symbolic ways—such as Castro's decision to forgo trips to Moscow—and in tangible ways, by seeking aid from several other countries. Cuba also ignored Soviet wishes to desist from supporting armed revolution in Latin America, which conflicted with the programs of Latin American Communist parties closely tied to Moscow. The crisis also made Cuba and the United States implacable enemies, a position that was solidified by Cuba's activities in the Latin American region.

The remainder of the decade can be characterized as a period of cold war between the two countries. There was little direct contact, and the contact that did occur served only to deepen the antagonisms. Despite Kennedy's apparent promise to Khrushchev, the United States maintained some support for the counterrevolutionaries who actively fought inside Cuba until 1966. The attempts on Fidel Castro's life also continued until at least 1965.[40] In 1970, the United States confronted the Soviet Union again, in a mini–missile crisis, over the construction of a submarine base at Cienfuegos. Soviet submarines had begun to make regular port stops in Cuba without U.S. protest. But the creation of a permanent facility led National Security Adviser Henry Kissinger to demand "quietly" that the base be dismantled, and the Soviets complied.[41]

U.S. attention in this period focused less on Cuba's ties with the Soviet Union and more on Cuba's activities in Latin America. The vision of "no more Cubas" led Kennedy to propose the Alliance for

Progress, a foreign assistance program intended to attack the poverty and corruption in the region on which revolution fed. Yet Kennedy sowed the seeds of the program's failure by coupling economic assistance with extensive military aid to create counterinsurgency programs against guerrilla groups. The military aid provided Latin American militaries with the means to suppress legitimate dissent as well as guerrillas, to stifle reform, and ultimately to stage coups against democratic regimes in the region.[42] In effect, by dwelling on Cuba and the fear that similar revolutionary regimes might emerge in other Latin American countries, Kennedy and Johnson undermined the U.S. interest in promoting democracy in the region.

Similarly, the anti-Cuba policy led to an expansion of U.S. covert activity in Latin America throughout the 1960s. It also prompted the United States to intervene in the Dominican Republic in 1965 with 22,000 troops, in response to a false alarm that the country was about to be taken over by communists.[43] To Latin Americans, these military actions harkened the specter of U.S. "gunboat diplomacy," and they undermined the moral stature of the United States in the hemisphere.

In effect, there were three major objectives of U.S. policy toward Cuba from 1959 to 1971: (1) to overthrow the Cuban government; (2) to isolate and "contain" Cuba; (3) to reduce the Soviet presence in Cuba. Initially, U.S. policymakers focused on the first goal. Isolation was one of several means to that end. By 1971 isolation and containment had become ends in and of themselves, apart from the objective of overthrowing the Cuban government, and Cuban ties to the Soviet Union became a primary consideration.[44]

The Roller Coaster Decade, 1971–1980

By the early 1970s, several factors coalesced to reduce the tension between Cuba and the United States. The Richard Nixon administration had fashioned as its hallmark détente with both the Soviet Union and China: Anticommunism was less in vogue. At the same time, Cuba had curtailed its practice of supporting armed revolution in the hemisphere and had begun to develop state-to-state relations with several Latin American countries.

The Vietnam War also had a multifaceted though indirect effect. Latin American leaders were more willing to risk independent positions in the 1970s, in part because they saw the United States consumed by its attention to Vietnam. In the United States, the war destroyed the post–World War II consensus, which had included a common view in the executive and legislative branches about the proper role for the United States in the Third World. As fundamental questioning about that role began to grow, policy toward Cuba became a natural object of attention.

A movement to relax the hostility between Cuba and the United States first began in Congress in 1971, and it gained force in the next three years.[45] In 1974 senators Claiborne Pell (D-R.I.) and Jacob Javits (R-N.Y.), along with several congressional aides, traveled to Cuba. Charles Whalen's (R-Ohio) 1975 trip was the first for a member of the House of Representatives since 1960, and it was followed by those of several other representatives and more senators. Members perceived that U.S. policy toward Cuba was hurting U.S. interests, both in Latin America and more generally in terms of U.S. prestige. The United States appeared isolated, whereas the intent of the policy had been the reverse—to isolate Cuba. A growing number of Latin American countries were breaking the trade embargo and calling for a change in the OAS prohibition on trade. To several key members of Congress involved in foreign affairs it seemed clear that the policy made the United States look like an ogre, which reinforced an image harmful to U.S. interests in the region.[46]

Although members of Congress acted independently and with some courage in light of persistent anti-Cuban rhetoric from President Nixon, the executive signaled its support for the congressional activities at key junctures. The United States signed an antihijacking treaty with Cuba in February 1973. In June 1974, during the waning days of President Nixon's tenure, Secretary of State Henry Kissinger gave approval for a trip to Cuba by Pat Holt, Senate Foreign Relations Committee chief of staff. Holt had requested permission to travel there more than a year before.

At about this time Kissinger also named William Rogers as assistant secretary of state for inter-American affairs. Rogers had served on the Linowitz Commission, a private group composed largely of business leaders and former government officials, which had advocated the normalization of relations with Cuba. By the end of 1974, Rogers was meeting with Cuban diplomats in New York, where Cuba has a mission to the United Nations (UN). He used these talks to assess the possibilities for negotiations on normalization. As the talks progressed, both the Cuban and U.S. delegations felt that discussions should occur in more appropriate surroundings—the two sides were meeting in semisecret locations, such as a coffee shop at New York's LaGuardia Airport. Thus in 1975, Rogers initiated a change in travel regulations for Cuban diplomats so that they could go beyond a twenty-five-mile limit from the UN and travel to Washington, D.C.

The United States also relaxed its position on the economic embargo against Cuba, which had been instituted in 1964. Several countries in the region already had broken the embargo and were carrying on extensive trade with Cuba. (Mexico had never participated in the embargo.) Others sought trade, and the Latin Americans had begun to view the embargo as a threat to their own sovereignty. U.S. policy barred corporations in Latin America from trading with Cuba if their parent corporation was based in the United States. Under pressure from Latin American countries, in 1975 the United States finally supported a majority in the Organization of American States by voting to lift the OAS embargo. Each country was permitted to trade with Cuba as it wanted, and the United States chose to continue its own embargo against Cuba. However, it did allow third-country subsidiaries of U.S. corporations to trade with Cuba.

Though a sharp contrast to Nixon's antagonistic posture toward Cuba, these efforts of the Gerald Ford administration to reduce tension were so tentative that they were quickly dashed by the war in Angola. Kissinger perceived Cuba to be thwarting U.S. interests there and saw little reason to "reward" Cuba with relaxed tension. By 1976 reports circulated through Washington of renewed Defense Department contingency plans for a military blockade of Cuba or even an attack.[47] In October, several terrorists—some of whom had been previously on the CIA payroll—blew up a Cuban civilian airplane, killing the seventy-three passengers. This led Cuba to abrogate the antihijacking agreement because it included provisions that mandated each country to try to prevent such attacks. Cuba charged that the United States had failed to comply with the agreement, because it had not warned Cuba of the terrorists' plans. Thus Jimmy Carter inherited a hostile atmosphere with respect to Cuba when he took office three months later.

The Carter administration moved quickly to reduce the tension. UN Ambassador Andrew Young characterized the Cuban presence in Angola as a "stabilizing" influence. Assistant Secretary of State Terence Todman traveled to Cuba in April 1977 to sign a fishing and maritime boundary agreement. He also negotiated a changed status for the diplomatic missions that represented U.S. interests in Cuba and Cuban interests in the United States. U.S. and Cuban diplomats began to staff the missions, respectively, in September 1977. The United States also facilitated tourist travel to Cuba, by easing currency restrictions and permitting charter flights. The Carter rapprochement, moreover, was reinforced by several members of Congress who resumed trips to Cuba in 1977 and introduced legislation to lift the bilateral U.S. embargo against Cuba.

Cuba responded to Carter administration overtures by agreeing to release a large number of political prisoners and by permitting them to emigrate to the United States. At the time Carter initiated his opening to Cuba, there were several thousand Cuban political prisoners. In 1979 the Cuban government released 3,600 of them.[48]

The U.S. government's relaxation of tourist restrictions encouraged a group of prominent Cuban exiles—called the Committee of 75—to initiate a dialogue with the Cuban government. Their discussions led to an unprecedented relaxation of immigration rules by Cuba, and several hundred thousand exiles returned to Cuba for family visits in 1979.[49] In part, the dialogue reflected an effort by Cuba to reach out to the Cuban-American community, and the results indicated that the community was not a solid phalanx in opposition to normalization.

However, by 1979 the warming trend in relations had been reversed. As they had during the Ford administration, United States and Cuban paths crossed in Africa, and the clash toppled the fragile structure that was being built toward normalization. To be sure, the improvement of relations with Cuba had not been universally endorsed throughout the U.S. government. As with any major initiative, some career officials, such as those in the Central Intelligence Agency, Department of Defense, and National Security Agency who had built their reputations over many years by advocating one policy, were loathe to see a change.[50] In this case, they were encouraged by Zbigniew Brzezinski, President Carter's special assistant for national security, to pursue their hostility to Cuba.[51] They encouraged the president, and other supporters of better relations, to perceive Cuban behavior through a lens that darkened its image and made Cuban actions appear intentionally harmful to U.S. interests, regardless of their true character. Ultimately, when differences arose between Cuba and the United States, the antagonists of normalization were then able to declare that their position had been valid all along.

Brzezinski focused on Africa, where he imprinted his East-West picture of the world with a special vehemence. Without an appreciation for the particular histories that led to regional conflicts, he believed that conflicts there reflected a bipolar struggle between the United States and the Soviet Union. Cuban or Soviet involvement with any antagonist in a struggle confirmed this view for him, and he attempted to manipulate the public perception and the official U.S. position to conform to his view.[52]

The 1977–1978 conflict between Ethiopia and Somalia over a border region called the Ogaden offered Brzezinski an opportunity to pursue his agenda.[53] From the moment it gained independence in 1960, Somalia had challenged Ethiopia's claim to the Ogaden, which dated back to the 1890s. The two countries, located in the strategic northeast corner of Africa, had fought over the area briefly in 1964.[54]

Both the United States and Soviet Union had vested some interest in the area. Until 1977, the United States had a base in Ethiopia and supplied it with weapons; the Soviet Union had a similar relationship with Somalia.[55] But a revolution in Ethiopia in 1974 began to unravel the relationships. In 1977 Somalia expelled the Soviets and Ethiopia expelled the United States, and in effect the two superpowers switched their allegiances.[56]

Meanwhile, in mid-1977 the Western Somalia Liberation Front (WSLF), an independence movement in the Ogaden, had mounted a serious effort to gain control of the territory from Ethiopia. The WSLF had been supplied with aid by Somalia, which sent its own troops into battle against Ethiopia in December 1977. In turn, Cuba and the Soviet Union increased aid to Ethiopia, and a large contingent of Cuban troops arrived early in 1978 to repel the Somali invasion.[57]

The United States backed Somalia quite cautiously, and the evidence of U.S. support for the invasion is ambiguous.[58] Indeed, Somalia had scant international endorsement for its action, and the Organization of African Unity implicitly backed Ethiopia's claim.[59] In this respect, Cuba's involvement was considered legitimate by a majority of African countries because its aid was requested by a sovereign country for defensive purposes. But Brzezinski seized upon the Cuban involvement as proof of his contention that Cuba was a surrogate force for Soviet penetration in Africa. Though he acknowledged in his memoirs that "[the Somalis] were the nominal aggressors in the Ogaden," he argued that "the situation between the Ethiopians and the Somalis was more than a border conflict. . . . It represented a serious setback in our attempts to develop with the Soviets some rules of the game in dealing with turbulence in the Third World. The Soviets had earlier succeeded in sustaining, through the Cubans, their preferred solution in Angola, and they now seemed embarked on a repetition in a region in close proximity to our most sensitive interests."[60] He proudly detailed, then, how he attempted to convince the media that accommodation with Cuba thus would undermine U.S. credibility with its allies in Africa.[61]

This view had only partial support inside the Carter administration. Calmer officials prevailed in late 1977, and the president did not confront Cuba over the Ogaden war. However, in the case of Zaire, President Carter went out on a limb in a verbal attack against Cuba.

In May 1978, a large group of Katangese exiles entered the Shaba (formerly Katanga) province of Zaire from Angola in an effort to recapture land on which they had once lived.[62] Zaire, a U.S. ally located in the heart of Africa, relied on the mineral wealth of Shaba province to sustain itself, so that loss of the province would have become a threat to Zaire's stability. President Carter became convinced that the invasion was instigated by Cuba, although the evidence indicated just the opposite—that Cuba had attempted to stop it.[63] He initially charged that the rebels were trained by Cuban forces in Angola, and later the president asserted that at the least, because Cuba knew about the invasion, it was blameworthy because it had not prevented the rebels from entering Shaba. Evidence for both charges proved unconvincing to the Senate Foreign Relations Committee, which found that the president's charges were overstated.[64] Yet this was a position from which he would not withdraw.

From then on, U.S.-Cuban relations grew increasingly tense as the Carter administration shifted its perspective of Cuba. The Brzezinski view, that Cuba was a surrogate of the Soviet Union and that any actions in which it was involved transformed the situation into an East-West battleground, prevailed. With that perspective, it was difficult to treat Cuba principally in bilateral terms. U.S.-Cuban issues became linked to U.S.-Soviet relations, and the administration became preoccupied with Cuba's international affairs, especially those with the Third World.

Cuba was scheduled to host the summit and to become the chair of the ninety-two-nation Non-Aligned Movement in late summer 1979. Eighteen months earlier, U.S. emissaries had attempted (unsuccessfully) to persuade the movement to shift the site of its meeting away from Havana. Just prior to the actual summit conference, the United States pressed its Third World allies to oppose Cuba's proposed draft of the summit declaration, which was strongly critical of the United States. Then in an apparent effort to discredit Cuba's leadership of the nonaligned countries, the Carter administration charged that an alleged 3,000-person Soviet combat brigade in Cuba posed a new threat to the United States.[65] Though it turned out to be a Soviet training group that had been stationed in Cuba since the 1962 missile crisis, President Carter demanded that the Soviets withdraw the brigade, and he ordered the creation of the Caribbean Joint Task Force, a small military unit on Key West, to counter the supposed danger.[66]

To underscore the official view that Cuba was once again a major enemy of the United States, the president issued a policy statement on Cuba, Presidential Directive 52, in October 1979. It ordered national security agencies "to devise strategies for curbing Cuba's activities [in the Third World] and isolating it politically."[67] These actions occurred as the Carter administration was confronted with what it perceived were several major foreign policy problems simultaneously. In March 1979, the New Jewel Movement overthrew the dictatorship of Eric Gairy on the eastern Caribbean island of Grenada. During the summer Grenada vociferously criticized the United States and warmly embraced Cuba, which sent aid missions there. In July, the Sandinista National Liberation Front deposed the Nicaraguan dictator Anastasio Somoza, and a week later a delegation of Sandinista leaders attended the July 26 celebrations in Havana. The Brzezinski wing of the Carter administration saw an arc of crisis in the Caribbean Basin, with Cuba at its apogee.

On top of these strains, the Mariel "boatlift" of April-May 1980 helped to raise U.S.-Cuban relations to the heights of tension they had been in earlier years. Approximately 120,000 Cubans emigrated from the port of Mariel when the Cuban government permitted essentially unrestricted exodus from the island, and the United States welcomed them. The administration charged that the Cuban government forced some prisoners and patients in mental institutions to emigrate at this time.[68]

At the end of 1980, the Carter administration thus bequeathed to the incoming Ronald Reagan administration an antagonistic relationship with Cuba. In addition, through the use of anti-Cuban rhetoric for two years, it effectively preconditioned the public for the hostile stance Reagan would take to Cuba. The halting efforts toward normalization by Ford and Carter left another legacy as well: a sense among policymakers that U.S. policy toward Cuba had failed to achieve U.S. objectives because it had been insufficiently harsh. John Ferch, head of the U.S. Interests Section in Havana from 1982 to 1985, described the feeling in 1983 when he remarked that "there is no doubt that the moderation of the Carter Administration was interpreted in Cuba as a sign of weakness."[69]

Carter's ultimate legacy to his successor, a legacy he had adopted from Ford, was an approach to the Cuban question that dictated that relations with Cuba were unimportant for their own sake; relations were desirable only to the extent that they might assist in the attainment of other international goals, especially those of an East-West nature. Thus the Ford administration had favored a move toward normalization of relations with Cuba in order to improve its relations with the rest of Latin America. As we have seen, the United States had become isolated in the OAS because of the Cuban embargo, and several countries that sought trade with Cuba demanded their subsidiaries of U.S. corporations be allowed to trade with Cuba. When the OAS ended the embargo in 1975 and the United States allowed third-country subsidiaries to trade with Cuba, the pressure for normalization ceased. At that very time, Cuba's long-standing involvement in Africa embroiled it in the Angola war. With no countervailing pressure, the Ford administration interpreted this in an East-West context and chose to close off the opening that had begun in 1974.

Similarly, the Carter administration hoped that the process of normalizing relations with Cuba could enable the United States to fashion a new policy with respect to the Caribbean and to establish a new, less hegemonic relationship with Latin America. Indeed, a Panama Canal Treaty and normalization of relations with Cuba were high on its hemispheric agenda. Officials such as UN Ambassador Andrew Young also reasoned that normal relations could help to promote peace in southern Africa and could contribute to an overall improvement in U.S. relations with Africa.[70] U.S. support for South Africa against Angola during the Ford administration had embittered black African countries, and Carter made the restoration of good relations with Africa a high priority. Considering Cuba's high standing on the continent, the move toward normalization would be a signal to Africa that the United States was changing course.

Because of Carter's approach, his Cuba policy became a victim of circumstances. The administration incurred heavy political costs to secure passage of the Panama Canal Treaty in 1977. Though the treaty had been negotiated largely by the Ford administration, conservative groups and legislators attacked Carter for "giving" the canal to the Panamanians. They used the treaty as a symbol for their general critique of Carter's human rights and détente policies, which made him more reticent about incurring similar costs for an accommodation with Cuba. Meanwhile, he was able to point to the treaty in dealings with Latin Americans as a symbol of his new approach to the region and could forgo the Cuba card for this purpose.

With respect to Africa, Carter used well several other ploys to improve relations with key countries. In fact, Africans viewed the administration's human rights policy as an antiapartheid policy; they appreciated the prominence given to Ambassador Young; stronger ties with Nigeria caused in part by major oil agreements, gave the United States an important ally that spoke up for U.S. interests. At the same time, Cuba's activities in Ethiopia received a less than enthusiastic African reception, though they were not overtly criticized.

Thus, Cuba policy took a roller coaster ride during the 1970s, as the potential benefits of normalization with Cuba seemed to be overshadowed by the costs. Indeed, from Kennedy through Carter policy toward Cuba was caught up in the large web of U.S. international interests.[71] Cuba was at the center of the missile crisis, but was excluded from negotiations between the United States and the Soviet Union. Concern about Cuba's role in Latin America stimulated the Alliance for Progress, but the United States maintained a cold war with Cuba during the period. And concerns about the eroding U.S. position in Latin America and Africa contributed to Ford's and Carter's moves toward normalization with Cuba. This approach was firmly in place when President Reagan took office, and he did little to unsettle it. One official in the Defense Department succinctly alluded to it in an interview when he said, "Our policy with respect to Cuba has really been a policy with respect to Central America. It's there that relations between the United States and Cuba will be played out."[72]

Notes

1. Abraham F. Lowenthal, "Ronald Reagan and Latin America: Coping with Hegemony in Decline," in *Eagle Defiant,* ed. Kenneth Oye, Robert Lieber, and Donald Rothchild (Boston: Little, Brown, 1983).

2. Philip S. Foner, *A History of Cuba and Its Relations With the United States* (New York: International Publishing Co., 1963), vol. 2, pp. 289–296; Jules Robert Benjamin, *The United States and Cuba: Hegemony and Dependent Development, 1880–1934* (Pittsburgh: University of Pittsburgh Press, 1977), pp. 4–5.

3. Hugh Thomas, *Cuba, or The Pursuit of Freedom* (London: Eyre & Spottiswoode, 1971), p. 466; Juan M. del Aguila, *Cuba: Dilemmas of a Revolution* (Boulder, Colo.: Westview, 1984), pp. 13–14; Benjamin, *The United States and Cuba,* pp. 7–9.

4. Thomas, *Cuba, or The Pursuit of Freedom,* chapters 30–33; and Lewis A. Perez, Jr., *Cuba Between Empires, 1878–1902* (Pittsburgh: University of Pittsburgh Press, 1983), chapters 7–10.

5. Benjamin, *The United States and Cuba,* p. 9.

6. Ibid., p. 10.

7. Louis A. Perez, Jr., *Cuba Under the Platt Amendment: 1902–1934* (Pittsburgh: University of Pittsburgh Press, 1986), p. 76.

8. The Platt Amendment officially was entitled, "Treaty Between the United States and Cuba Embodying the Provisions Defining the Future Relations of the United States with Cuba Contained in the Act of Congress," Ratified by the President, June 25, 1904, 56th Cong., 2nd Sess., Ch. 803. It declared that "the government of Cuba consents that the United States may exercise the right to intervene for the preservation of Cuban independence,

the maintenance of a government adequate for the protection of life, property, and individual liberty, and for the discharging of [U.S.] obligations . . . imposed by the Treaty of Paris [the treaty with Spain that ended the war]."

9. Perez, *Cuba Under the Platt Amendment,* chapter 5; Thomas, *Cuba, or The Pursuit of Freedom,* chapters 42, 44.

10. Benjamin, *The United States and Cuba,* p. 28; Arthur Downey, "United States Commercial Relations with Cuba: A Survey," reprinted as Appendix VI, U.S. Congress, House Committee on International Relations, "U.S. Trade Embargo of Cuba: Hearings on H.R. 6382," 94th Cong., 1st Sess., 1975, p. 586.

11. Jorge I. Dominguez, *Cuba: Order and Revolution* (Cambridge: Harvard University Press, 1978), p. 21.

12. Medea Benjamin et al., *No Free Lunch* (San Francisco: Institute for Food and Development Policy, 1984), pp. 9, 10.

13. Perez, *Cuba Under the Platt Amendment,* pp. 13–14.

14. Luis E. Aguilar, *Cuba 1933: Prologue to Revolution* (New York: Norton, 1974), chap. 8; Benjamin, *The United States and Cuba,* pp. 40–44.

15. Harold Molineu, *U.S. Policy Toward Latin America: From Regionalism to Globalism* (Boulder, Colo.: Westview, 1986), pp. 22–24.

16. Aguilar, *Cuba 1933,* chapters 5, 8, 9; Benjamin, *The United States and Cuba,* chapters 5, 6.

17. Benjamin, *The United States and Cuba,* chapters 7–9; Aguilar, *Cuba 1933,* chapters 10–16.

18. Downey, "United States Commercial Relations with Cuba," pp. 588, 621–622; Carmelo Mesa-Lago, *The Economy of Socialist Cuba: A Two-Decade Appraisal* (Albuquerque: University of New Mexico Press, 1981), p. 8.

19. Robert F. Smith, *The United States and Cuba: Business and Diplomacy, 1917–1960* (New York: Bookman Associates, 1960), chapter 10.

20. Dominguez, *Cuba,* chapter 3; Smith, *The United States and Cuba: Business and Diplomacy, 1917–1960.* Cuba's alliance with the United States during World War II contributed to the close ties.

21. Dominguez, *Cuba,* pp. 60–61.

22. Hugh Thomas, *The Cuban Revolution* (New York: Harper & Row, 1977), p. 3.

23. The July 26th Movement took its name from a failed attack by the organization against the army's Moncada Barracks in Santiago on July 26, 1953. The surviving members were jailed and later freed in a 1955 general amnesty Batista declared in order to appease U.S. critics of his regime's oppression. The movement reappeared in late 1956, setting up headquarters in the Sierra Maestra mountains. It should be noted that it had cool if not hostile relations with the Cuban Communist party (PSP), which opposed armed action until 1958.

24. Herbert L. Matthews, *Revolution in Cuba* (New York: Scribner's, 1975), pp. 81–85; Thomas, *The Cuban Revolution,* chapter 9.

25. Thomas, *The Cuban Revolution,* chapters 15, 18; Matthews, *Revolution in Cuba,* pp. 117–119.

26. For a probing examination of this question, see Saul Landau, "Asking the Right Questions About Cuba," in *The Cuba Reader,* ed. Philip Brenner, William LeoGrande, Donna Rich, and Daniel Siegel (New York: Grove, forthcoming).

27. Tad Szulc, *Fidel: A Critical Portrait* (New York: Morrow, 1986), p. 480.

28. Philip Bonsal, *Cuba, Castro and the United States* (Pittsburgh: University of Pittsburgh Press, 1971).

29. Thomas, *The Cuban Revolution,* chapters 33, 34; Matthews, *Revolution in Cuba,* chapters 6–8.

30. In 1959, smaller holdings of some U.S. companies were nationalized in return for the offer of twenty-year bonds. Private businesses continued to exist well into the 1960s.

31. Szulc, *Fidel,* pp. 488, 498; Dominguez, *Cuba,* p. 146. Also see D. Bruce Jackson, *Castro, the Kremlin and Communism in Latin America* (Baltimore: Johns Hopkins Press, 1969).

32. Peter Wyden, *Bay of Pigs: The Untold Story* (New York: Simon and Schuster, 1979) provides the best detailed study of the operation. For references to the president's authorization, see p. 25. Also see Matthews, *Revolution in Cuba,* pp. 190–206; Thomas, *The Cuban Revolution,* pp. 580–581.

33. Wyden, *Bay of Pigs,* p. 185.

34. U.S. Senate, Select Committee to Study Governmental Operations with Respect to Intelligence Activities, "Alleged Assassination Plots Involving Foreign Leaders," Report No. 94-465, 94th Cong., 1st Sess., November 20, 1975, pp. 71–180; Taylor Branch and George Crile III, "The Kennedy Vendetta," *Harper's,* August 1975; Warren Hinckle and William Turner, *The Fish Is Red: The Story of the Secret War Against Castro* (New York: Harper & Row, 1981).

35. Paul Hoeffel and Sandra Levinson, eds., *The U.S. Blockade: A Documentary History* (New York: Center for Cuban Studies, 1979); Philip Brenner, *The Limits and Possibilities of Congress* (New York: St. Martin's Press, 1983), p. 43.

36. Morris H. Morley, "Toward a Theory of Imperial Politics: United States Policy and the Processes of State Formation, Disintegration and Consolidation in Cuba, 1898–1978," Ph.D. Dissertation, State University of New York at Binghamton, 1980, chapter 11; E. T. Smith, *The Fourth Floor* (New York: Random House, 1962); William A. Williams, *The United States, Cuba, and Castro* (New York: Monthly Review Press, 1962); Carla Anne Robbins, *The Cuban Threat* (New York: McGraw-Hill, 1983), chapter 3.

37. Hoeffel and Levinson, *The U.S. Blockade,* p. 26.

38. Thomas, *The Cuban Revolution,* chapters 44 and 45; James G. Blight, Joseph S. Nye, Jr., and David A. Welch, "The Cuban Missile Crisis Revisited," *Foreign Affairs,* vol. 66, no. 1, Fall 1987, pp. 170–188; Herbert Dinerstein, *The Making of a Missile Crisis* (Baltimore: Johns Hopkins Press, 1976); Robert F. Kennedy, *Thirteen Days* (New York: Norton, 1969); Graham Allison, *Essence of Decision* (Boston: Little, Brown, 1971).

39. Szulc, *Fidel,* p. 585; William M. LeoGrande, "Cuba," in *Confronting Revolution,* ed. Morris J. Blachman, William M. LeoGrande, and Kenneth Sharpe (New York: Pantheon, 1986), p. 250.

40. Senate Intelligence Committee, "Alleged Assassination Plots," pp. 174–180; Hinckle and Turner, *The Fish Is Red.*

41. Robbins, *The Cuban Threat,* pp. 86–89; Henry Kissinger, *The White House Years* (Boston: Little, Brown, 1979), pp. 635–651.

42. Cole Blasier, *The Hovering Giant: U.S. Responses to Revolutionary Change in Latin America* (Pittsburgh: University of Pittsburgh Press, 1976), pp. 241–258; Molineu, *U.S. Policy Toward Latin America,* pp. 130–133. One spectacular success of the counterinsurgency effort came in 1967, when Bolivian troops—allegedly with the aid of the CIA—killed Ernesto "Che" Guevara. Guevara, who left Cuba in 1965, had been a leader of the July 26th Movement and one of the principal government officials after the revolution. See Matthews, *Revolution in Cuba,* pp. 277–285.

43. Abraham F. Lowenthal, *The Dominican Intervention* (Cambridge: Harvard University Press, 1972); Piero Glijeses, *The Dominican Crisis* (Baltimore: Johns Hopkins Press, 1978).

44. Jane Franklin, *Cuban Foreign Relations: A Chronology, 1959–1982* (New York: Center for Cuban Studies, 1984).

45. Brenner, *Limits and Possibilities of Congress,* pp. 45–52.

46. Ibid., pp. 52–63.

47. Fred Hoffman, "Pentagon Reviewing Plans for Action Against Cuba," *Miami Herald,* March 26, 1976.

48. Inter-American Commission on Human Rights, *The Situation of Human Rights in Cuba,* Seventh Report, October 4, 1983 (Washington: Organization of American States, 1983), p. 49. Wayne Smith explained that Castro's offer to release political prisoners in 1978 came at a point when the rapprochement had been derailed and that he attempted to get it back on track by offering to address one of the three major issues on the Carter administration's Cuba agenda. See Wayne S. Smith, *The Closest of Enemies* (New York: Norton, 1987), pp. 146–163. Yet, it appears that Castro believed that the Carter administration might be responsive to his overture on political prisoners because of its earlier rapprochement and that the offer to release prisoners might lead to talks on other issues. Had Carter been hostile from the start, there would have been no incentive for Castro to make a move about prisoners.

49. Due credit for the family reunification visits should be given to the Carter administration, which had negotiated successfully the release of political prisoners from Cuba. However, as Wayne Smith recalled, the Carter administration did not want to take any credit for the prisoner release. Instead, the Committee of 75 went to Cuba, met with Castro, and announced that Cuba would permit both family visits by exiles and the emigration to the United States by political prisoners. See Smith, *The Closest of Enemies,* pp. 161–162.

50. For an interesting discussion of this phenomenon, see Lowenthal, "Ronald Reagan and Latin America," especially pp. 322–323.

51. Smith, *The Closest of Enemies,* p. 100.

52. Zbigniew Brzezinski, *Power and Principle* (New York: Farrar, Straus & Giroux, 1983).

53. Smith, *The Closest of Enemies,* pp. 129–134.

54. Bereket Habte Selassie, *Conflict and Intervention in the Horn of Africa* (New York: Monthly Review Press, 1980), pp. 99–105; Marina and David Ottaway, *Ethiopia: Empire in Revolution* (New York: Africana/Holmes and Meier, 1978), p. 162. The dispute grew out of the artificial boundary lines imposed by colonial powers on the people in the region who had a common culture and language.

55. Fred Halliday and Maxine Molyneux, *The Ethiopian Revolution* (London: Verso, 1981), pp. 214–222, 237–245.

56. Ibid., pp. 245–246; Selassie, *Conflict and Intervention in the Horn of Africa,* p. 121.

57. William M. LeoGrande, *Cuba's Policy in Africa, 1959–1980,* Policy Papers in International Affairs, no. 13 (Berkeley: University of California, 1980), pp. 35–42; Selassie, *Conflict and Intervention in the Horn of Africa,* pp. 109–119; Nelson P. Valdes, "Cuba's Involvement in the Horn of Africa: The Ethiopian-Somali War and the Eritrean Conflict," in *Cuba in Africa,* ed. Carmelo Mesa-Lago and June S. Belkin, Latin American Monograph and Document Series, no. 3 (Pittsburgh: University of Pittsburgh Center for Latin American Studies, 1982), pp. 73–76.

58. Halliday and Molyneux, *The Ethiopian Revolution,* pp. 223–229; Robert F. Gorman, *Political Conflict on the Horn of Africa* (New York: Praeger, 1981), p. 70.

59. Ibid., pp. 116–117; Selassie, *Conflict and Intervention in the Horn of Africa,* p. 118.

60. Brzezinski, *Power and Principle,* p. 178.

61. Ibid., pp. 180–181. Also see Smith, *The Closest of Enemies,* pp. 122–127. In fact, Castro went to the region in March 1977 in a failed attempt to mediate the dispute between Ethiopia and Somalia. See Valdes, "Cuba's Involvement in the Horn of Africa," p. 68; Halliday and Molyneux, *The Ethiopian Revolution,* pp. 252–253; Ottaway, *Ethiopia,* p. 170.

62. They had crossed into Shaba in 1977 but were repelled with the aid of several countries, especially Belgium, France, and Morocco. See Smith, *The Closest of Enemies,* pp. 120–121; LeoGrande, *Cuba's Policy in Africa,* pp. 23–24.

63. Smith, *The Closest of Enemies,* pp. 137–140.

64. Bernard Gwertzman, "Carter's Case on Cuba Not Proved, Foreign Relations Chairman Says," *New York Times,* June 10, 1978; Karen DeYoung, "Castro Again Denies U.S. Charges of Complicity in Zaire Raid," *Washington Post,* June 13, 1978. Also see LeoGrande, *Cuba's Policy in Africa,* pp. 26–27.

65. Smith, *The Closest of Enemies,* pp. 182–185. Robert Shaplen, "A Reporter at Large: Alignments Among the Nonaligned," *New Yorker,* October 22, 1979, p. 145. The existence of the Soviet brigade was actually revealed

publicly by Senator Frank Church (D-Idaho) during the 1979 Labor Day weekend, apparently without consent from the administration. One National Security Council official claimed in an interview with me that the administration did not intend to release the information until its veracity had been further confirmed and had not intended the revelation to impact on the nonaligned summit being held that weekend.

66. Norman Kempster, "Carter Increases Military Capabilities in Caribbean," *Los Angeles Times,* October 2, 1979. It appears that the president felt compelled to respond to the revelation in a forceful fashion, in part to preserve some political credibility for the Senate fight over the SALT II treaty vote. See Don Oberdorfer, "Cuban Crisis Mishandled, Insiders and Outsiders Agree," *Washington Post,* October 16, 1979, p. A14.

67. Barry Sklar, "Cuba: Normalization of Relations," Archived Issue Brief #75030, U.S. Library of Congress, Congressional Research Service, January 13, 1980, p. 13; *New York Times,* October 17, 1979.

68. Barry Sklar, "The Cuban Exodus," in *The Cuba Reader,* ed. Brenner et al.

69. John Ferch, "Cuban-American Relations: The U.S. Perspective," Paper presented at the International Roundtable: United States in the 1980s, Center for the Study of the Americas, Havana, March 16, 1983 (Spanish version) p. 16 (author's translation).

70. Author's interview with Andrew Young, July 1976.

71. William LeoGrande, "Cuba Policy Recycled," *Foreign Policy,* no. 46, Spring 1982.

72. Interview with the author in October 1983. The official asked to remain anonymous.

CHAPTER 2

U.S. Policy in the 1980s

THOUGH RELATIONS BETWEEN Cuba and the United States already were tense at end of the Carter administration, the incoming Reagan administration charged full force ahead to heighten the tension. Several officials of the new government advocated harsh measures against Cuba even before they assumed office. Cuba quickly became the focal point of their anticommunist crusade.[1] From the start they pursued a "get tough" policy and were joined by others who shared their perspective. A strident and consistent theme quickly emerged that Cuba was an implacable enemy of the United States.[2]

Raising the Stakes

For much of the 1980s tension between the two countries was at its highest level since the Cuban missile crisis. Much of this can be traced to Reagan administration policy. As Wayne Smith, former head of the U.S. Interests Section in Havana, observed in 1982: "The [Reagan] Administration began by excluding normalization of relations even as a distant objective. . . . Its initial position was that the United States would not even talk to the Cubans until they ceased all interventionist activities in Latin America and withdrew their troops from Africa. If they refused to do so, Washington would exclude no option, including a U.S. blockade or invasion of Cuba."[3]

Indeed, the policy was conceived before the administration assumed power. In the summer of 1980, a private group of conservative policy analysts proposed a set of hostile actions toward Cuba, as part of a report that outlined a new U.S. policy for Latin America. The group, called the Committee of Santa Fe, was made up of people who soon gained direct influence over U.S. policy. Lewis Tambs, the report's editor, became U.S. ambassador to Colombia and then Costa Rica. His name initially had been floated as the choice for assistant secretary of state for the region, but moderate senators strongly opposed him. Roger Fontaine, one of the report's authors, became chief Latin American specialist on the National Security Council.

It is instructive to consider the Committee of Santa Fe's proposals on Cuba because Reagan administration officials privately said the report helped to frame their policy prescriptions:

> Havana must be held to account for its policies of aggression against its sister states in the Americas. Among those steps will be the establishment of a Radio Free Cuba. . . . If propaganda fails, a war of national liberation against Castro must be launched. The second alternative will be to encourage the Cubans to make a radical shift in their foreign policy. . . . We should make it clear that if the Cuban-Soviet alliance is ended, the United States will be generous. . . . Thus Havana must be presented with two clear options. It is free to choose either, but the United States must carry out the threat or the promise with equal vigor.[4]

Major policy statements by the administration made clear that "threat" was its favored route because Cuba was a mortal enemy. Secretary of State Alexander Haig established the orientation in a February 1981 declaration, saying that the United States must "deal with the immediate source of the problem [in El Salvador]—and that is Cuba."[5]

A few days later, a State Department White Paper described the war in El Salvador as a "textbook case of indirect armed aggression by Communist power through Cuba." As a result, Assistant Secretary of State-designate Thomas Enders said in June 1981 that the U.S. "will focus on the source of the problem. . . . Cuba has declared covert war on its neighbors—our neighbors. The U.S. will join with them to bring the costs of that war back to Havana."[6]

President Reagan himself was fond of describing Cuba as a threat to U.S. access to Caribbean sea-lanes, "our lifeline to the outside world."[7] The National Bipartisan Commission on Central America (the so-called Kissinger Commission) pointed to Cuba as the instigator and sustainer of guerrilla war in the region, which posed a vital threat to the strategic interests of the United States. It too proposed that "we must also bring home to Havana a due appreciation of the consequences of its actions."[8] More recently, the alleged Cuban threat inspired a 1985 joint State and Defense Department report, which asserted: "Cuba, Nicaragua, and the Soviet Union are the principal threats to democracy in Central America. . . . Working through its key proxy in the region, Cuba, the Soviet Union hopes to force the United States to divert attention and military resources to an area that has not been a serious security concern to the United States in the past."[9] This rhetoric has defined the framework of recent policy and shaped the public debate about Cuba.

To be sure, members of Congress also contributed to the bellicose U.S. stance. For example, an amendment to a 1982 supplemental appropriations bill sponsored by Senator Steven Symms (R-Idaho), declared that the United States is determined: (1) to prevent Cuba, "by whatever means necessary, including the use of arms," from extending its "aggressive or subversive activities" to other countries in the hemisphere; (2) to prevent in Cuba the creation of a military capability that could threaten the security of the United States; (3) to work with the OAS and "with freedom-loving Cubans to support the aspirations of the Cuban people for self-determination."[10] The Symms amendment not only castigated Cuba as an enemy; it outlined a strategy for responding to Cuba that paralleled the administration's own plans for dealing with the threat it had identified. These plans hearkened to the objectives of preceding administrations: to destabilize the Cuban government, and to isolate Cuba internationally.

Destabilization

No one in the Reagan administration actually believed that enforcing the economic embargo would bring Cuba to its knees, as the Kennedy administration had hoped. But there was some expectation—based on experiences of 1979 and 1980—that economic pressure could influence political and social dynamics within Cuba to U.S. advantage.

The 1979 influx of exile visitors to Cuba had unsettled the carefully crafted system for distributing scarce consumer goods, which had been based on a worker's need and served as a material incentive for outstanding job performance. Initially, many of the visitors brought gifts worth thousands of dollars from the United States. Shortly after the program began, however, the Cuban government sought to reap hard currency benefits from the visitors' generosity, and it required them to purchase gifts at special government stores in Cuba. Though Cuba gained more than $100 million, the plan generated discontent among most Cubans. They saw exiles purchasing goods inside Cuba that they were unable to buy. Some Cubans were able to obtain much-sought-after refrigerators, sewing machines, and clothing merely on the basis of having an exile-relative or by paying an inflated price on the black market. Finally, the apparent ability of the exiles to purchase so many goods fueled a desire common to many people in poor countries, that is, to make their own fortune in the United States. These factors contributed to the Mariel boatlift in 1980.

Looking back at this disruption, Reagan administration analysts believed in 1981 that the demand for consumer goods in Cuba was a source of vulnerability.[11] They reasoned that this weakness could be exacerbated with a more strictly enforced embargo, which might make it more difficult for Cuba to obtain consumer goods. Then, if the embargo forced the Cuban government to repress demands, the ensuing conflict could cost the government some legitimacy. Alternately, if it led Cuba to give more flexibility to small farmers or to private entrepreneurs, in the hope of increasing the production of consumer items, that might give these classes increased power.

As a consequence of this logic, a more strictly enforced embargo against Cuba became a weapon the administration used to harass and attack Cuba. As an early warning of its intention, the administration ousted a Cuban diplomat from Washington in February 1981 for allegedly violating the embargo. Despite strong denials from Cuba, the United States charged that the diplomat had arranged for U.S. companies to export goods to Cuba through third countries. By the end of 1981, in an attempt to reduce Cuba's trade links to nonsocialist countries, the Reagan administration threatened to confiscate any imported goods that contained Cuban nickel. The United States also pressured European allies not to renegotiate Cuba's outstanding loans and to deny it any new loans.[12]

The same reasoning that led to the tightened embargo in part brought about the creation of Radio Marti, which began operation on May 19, 1985. First proposed by the Committee of Santa Fe as Radio Free Cuba, it was embraced by the Reagan administration in 1981 as a means of exacerbating tensions within Cuba through propaganda broadcasts. In its original form, it was to be akin to Radio Liberty and Radio Free Europe and was to be housed in their agency, the Board for International Broadcasting. Congress forced the administration to administer the station as part of the Voice of America.

There is a fine line between attempting to generate internal pressure in a country for the purpose of improving conditions there— as the Reagan administration claimed it intended to do with the embargo and Radio Marti—and trying to undermine a government with the hope of overthrowing it. Although Radio Marti was not likely to destabilize the Cuban government (Cubans already received news broadcasts from the Voice of America and anti-Castro propaganda from Miami radio stations), it did represent an attack on Cuba and seemed to reflect a disposition toward overthrowing the government. Indeed, the official Cuban government statement linked it to the embargo and to similar "threats and aggression of all kinds from the United States."[13] Such an interpretation was not unreasonable in light of the sustained anti-Castro propaganda by the Reagan administration. If the Reagan administration would want to attack Cuba militarily, it would need the public to believe that Cuba was worthy of being overthrown, because of both its behavior toward its own people and the threat it represented to the United States.

When a giant characterizes a small state as an enemy and publicly threatens it, the small state has to be wary. It appears that this was minimally the reaction that the Reagan administration sought to elicit from Cuba. In March 1981, for example, Under Secretary of State Walter Stoessel, Jr., told the Senate Foreign Relations Committee that the administration had contingency plans to "shut off the [alleged] arms flow" between Cuba and El Salvador. At the same time Admiral Harry Train, commander of the U.S. Atlantic fleet, told reporters in Venezuela that the United States was capable of blockading Cuba militarily.[14] On October 30, the U.S. Navy began extensive maneuvers in the Caribbean. A week later, the *New York Times* reported that Secretary of State Haig "has been pressing the Pentagon to examine a series of options for possible military action in El Salvador and against Cuba and Nicaragua," including, with respect to Cuba "an invasion by American and possibly Latin American forces."[15] Six months later, in April 1982, the U.S. Navy demonstrated a show of force again in the Caribbean. Called "Ocean Venture 82," the three-week series of maneuvers involved 45,000 troops, 350 airplanes, and 60 ships. It included an exercise to evacuate noncombatants from the U.S. naval base at Guantanamo.[16]

The Reagan administration may not have intended to take direct military action against Cuba, and its threats and contingency plans may have been designed only to keep Cuba "off balance." Still, Cuba took them quite seriously. On October 31, 1981, it placed the country on full military alert, mobilized its reserves, and began to practice civil defense drills. *Granma,* the official Communist party newspaper, dramatically quoted from a speech given by Fidel Castro six weeks earlier: "We will save peace if its enemies know that we are prepared to die for it rather than yield to blackmail and fear."[17] Cuba also requested increased military aid from the Soviet Union and began to reorganize the island's defenses with a new militia.[18]

The U.S. invasion of Grenada in October 1983 sent a special shock throughout Cuba because of its close ties with Grenada. Deputy

Foreign Minister Ricardo Alarcon told the *Washington Post* that Cuba saw the Reagan administration using the invasion as a basis for "intervention elsewhere."[19] The military actions in Grenada appeared to coincide with administration statements about bringing the Central American war home to Cuba.

Isolation

The Reagan administration's policy in Central America has been rooted in the untenable assumption that revolution is akin to an infection. Like an infection, revolution is believed to be induced by an outside agent or germ and to be capable of spreading from one body to the next.[20] Cuba was seen as the source of infection in Central America. Having claimed Nicaragua as its victim, Cuba, in the Reagan administration's view, became a threat to neighboring countries.[21]

This germ theory has led to a corollary: The source of infection must be isolated both to prevent further contagion and to return Nicaragua to an uncontaminated state. Cuba, then, became a jus- tification for U.S. military activity in Central America: The United States would provide a "shield" against infection. In turn, the U.S. goal of maintaining hegemony in Central America necessitated a policy of isolating Cuba.[22] Indeed, a major impetus for the 1982 Caribbean Basin Initiative (CBI) was to reduce the poverty in the region, on which Cuba could supposedly build revolutionary strug- gles. The CBI was a proposal to aid Caribbean and Central American countries through an infusion of new development grants and a reduction in the U.S. tariffs on their products. The 1984 Kissinger Commission focused even more explicitly on the goal of preventing Cuban "expansion," and it advocated a major U.S. development program for Central America.[23]

The Caribbean Basin Initiative and the Kissinger Commission proposals recalled the Kennedy-Johnson efforts to deal with the Cuban problem through the Alliance for Progress. As in the 1960s, the Cuban model was portrayed as a failure and as alien to the traditions of the hemisphere. Like the Kennedy and Johnson ad- ministrations, the Reagan team, too, sought to make Cuba a pariah state. Speaking in December, 1984 about U.S. policy, the director of the State Department's Office of Cuban Affairs said: "For Cuba, the way back from its present alienation from the political democracy which is advancing throughout the hemisphere will be long and arduous. Havana may someday realize that its own best interests would be served if it again joined the American mainstream."[24]

The effort to isolate Cuba went beyond rhetoric. The United States encouraged Latin American countries to break the ties they had developed with Cuba in the 1970s. Jamaica and Colombia, which had recently elected conservative governments and which were in great need of U.S. assistance, complied and broke relations in 1981. Moreover, the tightened economic embargo was intended to isolate as well as to destabilize Cuba. Also in 1981, the United States successfully blocked Cuban participation in a major international development conference at Cancun, Mexico—despite the fact that Cuba was head of the Non-Aligned Movement. By refusing to attend if Cuba were invited, the United States sent a message to the Third World that a country could choose to deal with either Cuba or the United States, but not both.

In 1982, to underscore his portrayal of Cuba as a pariah nation and to offer anti-Castro Cuban-Americans a symbolic gesture, President Reagan, in effect, revoked permission for U.S. tourists to travel to Cuba. Relying on his authority under the Trading with the Enemy Act, he banned the expenditure of dollars in Cuba except by scholars, journalists, and Cuban exiles who wished to see their families.[25] The travel ban had little practical effect. Its purported rationale was to deny hard currency to Cuba, but the largest number of U.S. citizens spending money in Cuba had been exiles who were able to continue their travel there under the new regulations.

Growing Tension

During the Reagan administration's first term, Cuba returned verbal attacks against it with equivalent calumnies. For example, at a meeting of the Inter-Parliamentary Union held in Havana in 1981, Fidel Castro exclaimed that "the group that constitutes the main nucleus of the current U.S. Administration is fascist." The speech was unexpectedly harsh in view of the fact that the audience included a U.S. senator and representative who had resisted administration entreaties to stay at home.[26]

However, from 1981 to 1984, Cuba generally welcomed any possibility for negotiations with the United States.[27] In 1984, it also endorsed the Contadora principles and treaty, which were developed by Mexico, Venezuela, Panama, and Colombia as a means to end the conflicts in Central America. In related moves, Cuba supported proposals for an international peacekeeping force in El Salvador and for international inspections in Nicaragua. As Seweryn Bialer and Alfred Stepan noted in reporting on a 1982 Cuban offer to negotiate a "mutual restraint" with the United States, the signals for accommodation may have been "entirely tactical."[28] But Cuba's sincerity nonetheless created the possibility for the United States to satisfy some interests if it were willing to overcome its hostility and negotiate with Cuba.

The Reagan administration finally recognized the utility of negotiations in 1984, when Cuba indicated a willingness to discuss the return of 2,700 exiles who had entered the United States during the Mariel boatlift. In part, though, the administration agreed to talks with Cuba only after the U.S. Cuban community had pressured President Reagan to reach an accommodation on immigration problems. U.S. officials claimed the 2,700 were criminals and patients of psychiatric institutions who were ineligible for entry to the United States, and they demanded that Cuba repatriate them. Meanwhile, Cuba called upon the United States to permit entry to thousands of Cubans who had valid visas and were waiting to emigrate.

Until the summer of 1984, Cuba insisted that it would not consider the repatriation of any emigrants who had departed in the 1980 exodus. Then in the summer of 1984, prior to the Democratic party convention, the Reverend Jesse Jackson traveled to Cuba and obtained agreement from President Castro to open talks with the United States on immigration. Negotiations began during the fall presidential campaign, and an agreement was reached on December 14, 1984. It specified that 2,746 exiles were to be returned to Cuba, and that each year 20,000 Cubans would be able to emigrate to the United States.[29]

Fidel Castro characterized the pact as a "constructive and positive" sign that could lead to negotiations in other areas of mutual interest. In contrast, the United States downplayed its significance. Secretary of State George Shultz disputed Castro's positive assessment by terming it "a lot of rhetoric." He added that "what we look for is some change in his behavior. And his behavior is to continue to try to export revolution all over the hemisphere."[30] The secretary's response followed the pattern of the previous four years, when the Cubans had tried to encourage some dialogue and the United States rebuffed the overtures.[31]

The Reagan administration's refusal to acknowledge the immigration accord as a step toward reduced tension contributed to the increase in tension that occurred in 1985. On May 19 the United States started broadcasts over Radio Marti, a medium-wave station aimed at creating dissension within Cuba. The station's programs, for example have included stories intended to discourage people from serving in Angola—by reporting unfounded charges that thousands of Cuban soldiers have been killed there and many also have contracted the AIDS virus.

Radio Marti had been authorized by the U.S. Congress in 1983; therefore, its inauguration came as no surprise to the Cuban government. Indeed, Cuba had threatened to overpower domestic U.S. broadcasts with a 300,000-watt signal on the 1040 AM frequency in retaliation for Radio Marti, and once, in 1984, demonstrated such a capability. The Cuban government also recognized that the station may have been no more than a symbolic reward to the anti-Castro Cuban-American community, which had supported Ronald Reagan's 1980 presidential campaign. Nonetheless, Cuba treated the opening of Radio Marti as a hostile assault and reacted to it with great anger. In part, the Cuban assessment was based on the Reagan administration's negative comments about Cuba after the two countries had signed the December 1984 immigration agreement.

Within hours of Radio Marti's first broadcast, Castro suspended the immigration agreement, and he announced Cuba would no longer permit Cuban exiles to visit the country.[32] In response, Reagan issued a proclamation that barred entry into the United States by any officer of the Cuban government or Cuban Communist party, or by individuals "considered by the Secretary of State . . . to be officers or employees of the Government of Cuba or the Communist Party of Cuba."[33] In effect, the proclamation provided the authority to bar virtually any Cuban, including scholars, artists, journalists, and students, and the administration used it to close the door on contact in the United States between Cuban and U.S. residents.

In July 1986 Cuba indicated an interest in restoring the immigration agreement. It proposed talks linking the restoration of the agreement to a new set of accords that would govern reciprocal radio broadcasts between Cuba and the United States. In effect, Cuba offered a way to reduce tension between the countries. It would be willing to back down from its earlier stance and to accept Radio Marti if Cuba could send radio broadcasts over an AM frequency to the United States. Negotiations over the Cuban plan lasted one day and ended when U.S. officials walked out. The State Department charged that Cuba "insisted on proposals that would have required major and disruptive changes in the organization of radio broadcasting in the United States." Cuba claimed that its position, which called for a "clear" channel, was merely a bargaining stance and not its final offer.[34]

By the fall of 1987 Cuba had dropped its insistence on linking the immigration agreement to radio broadcasts, and the two countries announced the restoration of the migration accord on November

20.[35] This came at the end of a year, though, in which there was a sense shared by officials in Havana and Washington that relations were at their lowest ebb since the 1962 missile crisis.[36]

As 1987 began, Cuba denied U.S. diplomats the right to land cargo charter planes, which made their shipment of cars, office equipment, and similar large items more difficult. In March, the United States aggressively pursued passage of a resolution in the UN Human Rights Commission that accused Cuba of persecuting political dissenters. It failed when Latin American members of the commission supported Cuba. Then in July Cuba aired a television documentary that detailed in an unprecedented fashion espionage activities by personnel in the U.S. Interests Section. Though Cuba did not demand the departure of any officials, four of whom were still working at the interests section when the program was televised, the United States retaliated by requesting two diplomats in the Cuban Interests Section in Washington to leave the country.[37] Throughout the year, then, the two countries responded to each other in ways that deepened the mutual distrust that was an inevitable by-product of the Reagan administration policy. The renewed immigration pact was a respite from the tension, but neither side characterized it as an opening for further accommodations.

Consequences of the Policy

Distrust was not the only consequence of the Reagan administration's policy toward Cuba. U.S. hostility had made it more difficult for Cuban-Americans to sustain contact with their families in Cuba. When Radio Marti went on the air, the Cuban government cut back to seventy-five per month the number of visas it was willing to issue exiles.

The policy also jeopardized the right of U.S. nationals to travel and to have a free exchange of ideas. President Reagan's 1985 proclamation led to the suspension of several university exchange programs. Though U.S. scholars were still invited to Cuba, the programs were not viable because U.S. officials refused visas for Cuban scholars to come to the United States. Cubans were barred, as well, from scholarly conferences in the United States, and Cuban poets, writers, and filmmakers were denied permission to lecture at U.S. universities.

The effect of these actions was to deny accurate information about Cuba to the U.S. public. Though administration officials denied this was their intention, the Treasury Department had attempted to restrict information from Cuba early in the Reagan administration. In May

1981 it began to block delivery of Cuban newspapers and magazines and announced it would strictly enforce a 1963 rule that banned the importation of publications from Cuba without a license. Officials relaxed the ban in 1982, but only after a lawsuit challenged the constitutionality of the Treasury Department action.[38]

By denying U.S. tourists the right to travel to Cuba and closing the door to Cuban intellectuals, the Reagan administration became freer to manipulate U.S. public opinion about Cuba. Fewer opposing views were available, and reduced contact between the citizens of both countries made it easier for the administration to depict Cuba with diabolical images. As a consequence, it has become more difficult for public officials to discuss U.S. policy toward Cuba in nonemotional terms, or to help people assess the objectives and viability of the current policy. The policy against Cuba in effect became a policy against open public debate about Cuba in the United States.

Notes

1. Philip Brenner, "Waging Ideological War: Anti-Communism and U.S. Policy in Central America," *The Socialist Register 1984* (London: Merlin Press, 1984), pp. 247–251.

2. For good reviews of the first two years of administration policy, see William LeoGrande, "Cuba Policy Recycled," *Foreign Policy,* no. 46, Spring 1982, and Max Azicri, "Cuba and the United States: What Happened to Rapprochement?" in *The New Cuban Presence in the Caribbean,* ed. Barry B. Levine (Boulder, Colo.: Westview, 1983).

3. Wayne S. Smith, "Dateline Havana: Myopic Diplomacy," *Foreign Policy,* no. 48, Fall 1982, pp. 159–160.

4. Lewis Tambs, ed., "A New Inter-American Policy for the Eighties: Report of the Committee of Santa Fe" (Washington, D.C.: Council for Inter-American Security, 1981), pp. 46–47.

5. Jane Franklin, *Cuban Foreign Relations: A Chronology 1959–1982* (New York: Center for Cuban Studies, 1984), pp. 36–37.

6. "Reagan Administration Policy Toward Cuba Takes Shape," *Cuba Update,* Center for Cuban Studies, July 1981, pp. 1–2.

7. "Text of Reagan [April 27, 1983] Address on Central America," *Congressional Quarterly Weekly Report,* April 30, 1983, p. 853.

8. *Report of the National Bipartisan Commission on Central America* [hereafter, Kissinger Commission], Washington, D.C., 1984, p. 122.

9. U.S. Departments of State and Defense, "The Soviet-Cuban Connection in Central America and the Caribbean," Washington, D.C., March 1985, pp. 1–2.

10. *Congressional Record,* August 10, 1982, p. S10088. The Senate passed the amendment by a vote of 68 to 28, and the House concurred in conference.

However, earlier in the year, thus further away from the midterm election, the resolution had been rejected by the Senate Foreign Relations Committee.

11. Cuba saw the same thing, and after 1980 significantly increased the availability of consumer goods. See Alfonso Chardy, "Open Market Lets Resurgent Havana Dress for Success," *Miami Herald,* March 25, 1985; Medea Benjamin et al., *No Free Lunch* (San Francisco: Institute for Food and Development Policy, 1984), chapter 5.

12. John M. Goshko, "U.S. Acts to Tighten Cuban Embargo," *Washington Post,* April 20, 1982, p. 1A; Helga Silva, "Tightening the Embargo," *Miami Herald,* September 5, 1982, p. 1F.

13. "Statement by the Government of Cuba," May 19, 1985, Cuban Interests Section, Washington, D.C.

14. Franklin, *Cuban Foreign Relations,* p. 38.

15. Leslie Gelb, "Haig Is Said to Press For Military Options for Salvador Action," *New York Times,* November 5, 1981, p. 1.

16. Philip Brenner, "U.S.-Cuba: Ambiguous Signals," *CubaTimes,* Summer 1982, p. 8; Azicri, "Cuba and the United States," p. 178. In June 1982 the U.S. Navy announced that it would reopen a facility on Key West—90 miles from Cuba—to provide a "forward operating base" for exercises in the Caribbean and other "contingencies." See Michael Getler, "Navy to Upgrade Key West Station for Capacity Near Cuba," *Washington Post,* June 10, 1982, p. A13.

17. Franklin, *Cuban Foreign Relations,* p. 44.

18. Ibid., p. 54; U.S. Departments of State and Defense, "The Soviet-Cuban Connection in Central America and the Caribbean," p. 9; H. Michael Erisman, *Cuba's International Relations* (Boulder, Colo.: Westview, 1985), pp. 149–150.

19. Edward Cody, "Cuba, Reading a Warning in Grenada Invasion, Alters Tone," *International Herald Tribune,* March 23, 1984; also, "Around the Americas: Cubans Stage Practice for a U.S. Invasion," *Miami Herald,* August 21, 1984.

20. For a good critique of the administration's assumptions, see Morris J. Blachman, Douglas C. Bennett, William M. LeoGrande, and Kenneth E. Sharpe, "The Failure of the Hegemonic Strategic Vision," in *Confronting Revolution: Security Through Diplomacy in Central America,* ed. Morris J. Blachman, William M. LeoGrande, and Kenneth Sharpe (New York: Pantheon, 1986), especially pp. 339–341.

21. U.S. Departments of State and Defense, "The Soviet-Cuban Connection," pp. 8–10, 37–38.

22. Alfonso Chardy, "U.S. Official Outlines Plan to Isolate Havana Regime," *Miami Herald,* November 29, 1983, p. 14A. Assistant Secretary of State Thomas Enders summarized the prevailing view in 1981: "Our response to the Cuban challenge is clear. *First,* we will help threatened countries to defend themselves." For the same reason, he added, "we will help countries in the [Caribbean] Basin to achieve economic success." *Cuba Update,* July 1981, p. 1 (emphasis is his).

23. Kissinger Commission, pp. 25–38. Also see Alfonso Chardy, "Proposed Literacy Campaign Would Counter Cuban Efforts," *Miami Herald,* January 31, 1984.

24. Kenneth Skoug, "The United States and Cuba," Current Policy No. 646, December 17, 1984, U.S. Department of State, Bureau of Public Affairs, p. 5.

25. Aaron Epstein, "Supreme Court Says President Can Limit Civilian Travel to Cuba," *Miami Herald,* June 29, 1984. See also, Azicri, "Cuba and the United States," pp. 180–181.

26. Christopher Dickey, "Castro Blasts Reagan at Global Conference," *Washington Post,* September 16, 1981; Philip Brenner, "U.S.-Cuba: Tension Mounts," *CubaTimes,* Fall 1981.

27. Smith, "Dateline Havana: Myopic Diplomacy," p. 161. Also see Leslie H. Gelb, "Cuban Calls for Talks With the U.S. and Accepts Part Blame for Strains," *New York Times,* April 6, 1982, p. A14.

28. Seweryn Bialer and Alfred Stepan, "Cuba, the US, and the Central American Mess," *New York Review of Books,* May 27, 1982, p. 18.

29. Joanne Omang, "U.S., Cuba End 4-Year Quarrel Over Refugees," *Washington Post,* December 15, 1984; "Estimate of Cuban Arrivals," *Miami Herald,* December 24, 1984.

30. Leonard Downie, Jr., and Karen DeYoung, "Cuban Leader Sees Positive Signs for Ties in Second Reagan Term," *Washington Post,* February 3, 1985; "Around the Americas: Shultz Dismisses Castro Overtures, Tells Managua to Change Behavior," *Miami Herald,* February 15, 1985, p. 22A. Also see Skoug, "The United States and Cuba," p. 5; "Cuba's 'Signals' for Talks Aren't Valid, U.S. Says," *Miami Herald,* January 31, 1985.

31. Wayne S. Smith, *The Closest of Enemies* (New York: Norton, 1987), pp. 249–260. In a 1984 interview with Knight-Ridder editors, President Reagan remarked that early in his administration, "We immediately picked up on [Cuban signals for negotiations] and then found that they evidently didn't mean it. . . . And they're making something of the same kind of noises now. . . . We don't think that they're really serious." See "Soviets, Cuba, Economy: What the President Said," *Miami Herald,* February 14, 1984. U.S. antipathy to negotiations with Cuba was made clear in a 1983 speech by John Ferch, head of the U.S. Interests Section in Havana. He contended that because "the recognition of 'the legitimacy of wars of national liberation' is incorporated in the Cuban constitution," Cuba has made itself an outlaw nation. The United States, he said, believes it is inappropriate to normalize relations with outlaws. See John Ferch, "Cuban-American Relations: The U.S. Perspective," Paper presented at the International Roundtable: United States in the 1980s, Havana, Center for the Study of the Americas, March 16, 1983 [Spanish version], p. 5 (translation by author). For similar comments by Ambassador Vernon Walters, see Don Bohning, "Envoy List U.S. Terms to Improve Cuba Ties," *Miami Herald,* January 7, 1983.

32. R. A. Zaldivar, "Castro Retaliates for Radio Marti," *Miami Herald,* May 21, 1985. Subsequently the Cuban government relaxed its position

slightly and granted seventy-five visas per month to exiles who wanted to visit their families in Cuba.

33. Ronald Reagan, "Suspension of Entry as Nonimmigrants by Officers or Employees of the Government of Cuba or the Communist Party of Cuba," Proclamation 5377, October 4, 1985, *Weekly Compilation of Presidential Documents,* vol. 21, no. 41, October 14, 1985, p. 1210. Exception was made for officials entering for the exclusive purpose of conducting business at the Cuban Interests Section in Washington, at the United Nations, or at the Cuban Mission to the United Nations in New York.

34. R. A. Zaldivar, "U.S.-Cuban Immigration Talks Fail," *Miami Herald,* July 11, 1986, p. 1; and interviews with Cuban officials in July 1987.

35. Neil A. Lewis, "U.S. and Havana Agree to Restore Immigration Pact," *New York Times,* November 21, 1987, p. 1.

36. Based on interviews with U.S. State Department and Cuban Ministry of Foreign Relations officials. Also see Flora Lewis, "U.S.-Cuba Cold Front," *New York Times,* February 27, 1987, p. A27; Joseph B. Treaster, "Downward Spiral for U.S.-Cuba Ties," *New York Times,* May 2, 1987, p. 1.

37. Peter Slevin, "Geneva Panel Derails Vote on Cuban Abuses," *Miami Herald,* March 12, 1987, p. 1; Lewis Duiguid, "Cuba Exults That CIA's Men in Havana Were Double Agents," *Washington Post,* July 27, 1987, p. A15; Lourdes Meluza, "U.S. Boots 2 Cuban Diplomats," *Miami Herald,* July 16, 1987, p. 1.

38. Franklin Siegel, "Treasury Impounds Cuban Periodicals," *CubaTimes,* Fall 1981, pp. 7–8.

CHAPTER 3

Issues in Contention

A LARGE SET OF BILATERAL and multilateral issues divide the United States and Cuba today. Bilateral issues are those that arise from the direct relationship between the two countries. Multilateral issues derive from differences they have that involve a third country. Given the relative sizes of Cuba and the United States, it is understandable that Cuba emphasizes bilateral disagreements because it views the United States as a direct threat. The United States emphasizes Cuba's relationships with other countries because it is through these relationships that the United States perceives its interests are affected.[1]

These contrasting emphases only begin to suggest the chasm that exists between the United States and Cuba. A review of the various issues each side has articulated makes clear that the current set of U.S. demands goes well beyond any negotiating table, for the United States in effect is demanding fundamental changes in Cuba and in Cuba's international relationships. Indeed, the U.S. position seems calculated to preclude any meaningful talks between the two countries. Cuba, in contrast, has listed a set of demands that are amenable to negotiation.

U.S. Demands

Multilateral Issues

The United States has focused its agenda of demands on Cuba's relationship with the Soviet Union, on Cuban support for both the Nicaraguan government and the guerrillas in El Salvador, and on the presence of Cuban troops in Angola. In each of the three cases, it has called for basic changes in Cuba's relationships.

Relations with the Soviet Union. The "bond" between the Soviet Union and Cuba, John Ferch said in 1983, "and the Soviet military and intelligence services in Cuba represent a considerable threat to the United States and its security."[2] This "special relationship with the Soviet Union," Kenneth Skoug asserted in 1984, is "the first and most critical" concern for the United States in considering relations with Cuba. It is a relationship, he added, on which the Reagan administration does not believe the United States can have much influence. Hence Skoug saw little basis for negotiating with Cuba.[3]

Cuba has never considered the U.S. concern about the Soviet presence to be a legitimate issue. The 1962 Kennedy-Khrushchev agreement, under which the Soviet Union agreed not to place offensive weapons in Cuba, and the 1970 accord, by which the Soviet Union agreed not to base nuclear submarines there, were made solely between the two superpowers. Cuba asserts that as a sovereign nation it can invite a foreign power to send forces to the island for defensive purposes, and it does have this right under the United Nations Charter.

For the United States, the issue is one of security, because the foreign power that Cuba would invite is the Soviet Union. President Carter raised the issue prominently in 1979, when he erroneously claimed that the Soviets had placed a new combat brigade in Cuba. From time to time in the 1980s unsubstantiated allegations have surfaced in Washington that Cuban MIGs have been reconfigured to make them capable of carrying nuclear weapons. U.S. fears were aroused further in 1985 when President Castro told the *Washington Post* that in light of threatening pronouncements by Reagan administration officials, Cuba contemplated the possibility of requesting offensive Soviet weaponry. Castro said that from Cuba's vantage point, it appeared that the United States no longer felt bound by the 1962 agreement.[4] However, since then the Cuban president has not repeated this contention, and Cuba has no offensive weapons.

Central America. Administration officials regularly link Soviet and Cuban relations to their concerns about Central America. In part, they allege, Soviet military assistance has given Cuba the wherewithal to provide support for revolutionary struggles in the region. It also adds a global strategic dimension to the local conflicts because Soviet bases in Central America, they say, could endanger the ability of the United States to respond appropriately to threats to its international interests.[5]

Whereas there is some evidence that Cuba, among other countries, provided advice, training and material assistance to Salvadoran guerrillas prior to 1981, there is little information about the extent of

Cuba's support and virtually no corroboration for the charge that it has continued to provide material aid. Indeed, Cuba has tended to act cautiously in Central America, in part because it fears a direct confrontation with the United States and in part because it does not want to offer the United States an excuse to send in U.S. troops. Cuba claims it has fewer than 1,000 military personnel in Nicaragua, and it removed 100 of these in early 1985.[6] U.S. estimates, which tend to include doctors and teachers, have varied from 3,000 to 9,000. The United States argues that the Cuban presence in Nicaragua provides the base for the military buildup there, which the United States asserts threatens the other countries in the region.

Nicaragua has said it must be prepared for a U.S. invasion, and it points to the U.S. military buildup in the region, which is more plausibly a threat to Nicaraguan security.[7] Cuba has contended that the conflicts in Central America can be settled only through multilateral negotiations, such as those led by Costa Rican President Oscar Arias in 1987 or by the Contadora countries between 1983 and 1986. It has agreed to abide by accords that result from a Central American peace plan, including the removal of any military forces. It should be noted that Castro strongly encouraged Nicaraguan President Daniel Ortega to comply with the Arias peace plan signed on August 7, 1987, by the Central American countries.[8]

Angola. Initially, President Carter acquiesced in the view that Cuban troops in Angola were a "stabilizing" influence, as Ambassador Andrew Young maintained, and that they had been sent to support the Popular Movement for the Liberation of Angola (MPLA) in 1975 only after South Africa invaded Angola, as veteran diplomat Wayne Smith reported.[9] They became a source of grievance after Carter's verbal altercation with Castro over the 1978 invasion of Zaire's Shaba province by rebels stationed in Angola. The Reagan administration inherited this issue when it took office and added a new twist. It endorsed the South African demand for the removal of Cuban troops from Angola as a precondition for the withdrawal of South African troops from Namibia. The United States argues that the Cuban presence in Angola is the sole stumbling block to an agreement on Namibian independence despite South Africa's occupation of its neighbor in violation of UN Security Council Resolution 435.

Until its third party congress in February 1986, Cuba had said that it would be willing to call home its estimated 25,000 to 30,000-person force on the basis of a November 1984 agreement it had reached with Angola.[10] This agreement specified that Cuban troops would depart when UN Resolution 435—which called for the withdrawal of South African troops from Namibia—was implemented and

after South Africa had withdrawn its troops from Angola and suspended aid to the National Union for the Total Independence of
Angola (UNITA) guerrillas. At that point, under the agreement, Cuba
would carry out in phases the removal of its troops, though Castro
later suggested that up to 10,000 soldiers might remain to guard
airports, the capital, and the Chevron/Gulf oil operations in Cabinda.[11]

In his closing address to the party congress, Castro went even
further and linked the withdrawal of Cuban troops to the end of
apartheid in South Africa. "There is," he said, "a perfect and very
just formula in Angola. If U.N. Resolution No. 435 is applied and
if apartheid is suspended, on the following day, the Cuban troops
begin their total withdrawal from Angola."[12] A few months later, at
the eighth summit of the Non-Aligned Movement in Zimbabwe, he
repeated this link between the end of apartheid and Cuban troop
withdrawal.[13]

However, in August 1987, after talks on normalization of relations
between the United States and Angola had broken down, there were
reports that Cuba and Angola had agreed to a new set of conditions
under which Cuban troops would depart.[14] Cuba has always made
clear that it would be willing to remove its troops at the request
of the Angolan goverment.[15] It appears that the possibility of relations
with the United States may have prompted Angola to seek a new
agreement with Cuba.

Bilateral Issues

Though several issues have occupied a place on the U.S. bilateral
agenda, the Reagan administration has highlighted three of them:
unsettled claims for expropriated property, Cuban support for Puerto
Rican independence, and human rights in Cuba.

Unsettled Claims. Since the break in relations between Cuba and
the United States, the United States has advanced the claims of its
citizens who allege that the Cuban government expropriated their
property without due compensation.[16] In 1972, the U.S. Foreign
Claims Settlement Commission certified claims against Cuba of $1.85
billion, which in 1987, with accrued interest, had grown to over $5
billion. The operative claim is probably smaller due to losses already
covered by income tax deductions, insurance payments, and the de
facto sale of claims to speculators. Cuba has said it would be willing
to negotiate this issue, and it has repaid claimants from Canada,
Switzerland, France, and Spain. It also has counterclaims against
the United States for the losses incurred during the covert war and
as a consequence of the embargo.

Puerto Rico. As with the question of a Soviet military presence in Cuba, the Cuban government has never recognized that its support for the independence of Puerto Rico is a legitimate bilateral issue with the United States. Cuban support for Puerto Rican independence dates back to the nineteenth century, prior to the time that the United States gained control over the island. Cuba views its efforts in the UN Committee on Decolonization and at the summits of the Non-Aligned Movement to be an international matter because it argues that Puerto Rico is not a part of the United States.[17]

Conversely, the United States claims Puerto Rico's status is an internal matter, especially in light of electoral outcomes that give little support to those who favor independence. It views Cuban initiation of proindependence resolutions with hostility. In addition, though the evidence to support the charge is flimsy, there have been claims that Cuba has aided proindependence guerrilla actions.[18] The formal U.S. demand has been that Cuba cease its support, in whatever form, of the independence movement.

Human Rights. Since the start of the Carter administration, a demand for the improved protection of human rights in Cuba has been on the U.S. agenda. Release of political prisoners was the main focus of the demand in the 1970s.[19] During the Reagan administration the demand expanded to cover unsubstantiated allegations about violations that involve torture and unwarranted detention, as well as the denial of the freedoms of speech, religion, and the press. Cuba has denied charges of torture and contends that human rights is not an appropriate issue for discussion prior to normalization of relations. It also emphasizes that its conception of human rights differs from that of the United States. Cuba places its highest priority on universal access to quality health care, housing, and sufficient food, and it considers such access to be a fundamental right.

Minor Problems. The three minor issues on the U.S. agenda would likely be resolved if there were agreement on more important differences between the two countries. The first demand is that Cuba improve the access and information it has given to consular officials in cases that involve alleged criminal activity by U.S. citizens. The second, which relates to U.S. allegations that Cuba has been involved in the Miami drug trade, is that Cuba tighten the patrol of its coastal waters with an eye to preventing the transportation of illegal substances.[20] In reality, Cuba has pursued drug dealers vigilantly, and nearly all of the U.S. citizens in Cuban jails are there on drug-related charges. Finally, the United States has demanded that Cuba cease interference with U.S. radio transmission, which is an issue with special poignancy in light of the inauguration of Radio Martí.

Cuban Demands

International Issues

Cuba has stated that it would be willing to negotiate its differences with the United States over international issues in the manner of normal sovereign states. It maintains that these matters are not appropriate for consideration as part of the discussions related to the process of normalizing relations. Cuba identifies its differences with the United States in terms of the roles of the two countries in Central America, the activities of each in Africa, proposals for Third World development, and each country's position in international forums. Its agenda of bilateral issues contains five items: Radio Marti, the economic embargo, terrorism and subversion, violation of Cuban airspace, and the naval base at Guantanamo.

Bilateral Issues

Radio Marti. The Cuban government perceives the series of propaganda broadcasts on the one AM and two shortwave bands that constitute Radio Marti as far more sinister than the mere distribution of foreign propaganda to its citizens. It considers Radio Marti to be an attack against its sovereignty and security. In part, this stems from Cuba's history with Radio Swan, which were CIA propaganda broadcasts used as a prelude to the Bay of Pigs invasion.[21] Its concern has been aroused in part because of the genesis of Radio Marti in the proposals from the Committee of Santa Fe. That 1980 report, by a group of conservatives who, as we have seen, gained policymaking posts in the administration, suggested that a propaganda station should be created as the first step in "a war of national liberation against Castro."[22] From the time the station was officially proposed, Cuba has made clear its opposition to Radio Marti. Cuba's anger over Radio Marti has thus raised it to the primary position as a source of grievance against the United States. Indeed, U.S. officials have acknowledged that its initiation moved relations between the two countries "back to square one."[23]

Embargo. In the 1960s Cuba viewed an end to the economic embargo as a vital necessity. Today it has more symbolic than practical significance. The Reagan administration's efforts to tighten the embargo—by pressuring Western European creditors to deny new loans and forbidding the purchase of products that contained Cuban nickel—did create the potential to harm the Cuban economy. And it was troublesome enough to warrant the creation of "dummy" corporations in third countries that would enable Cuba to circumvent the trade barriers. But the embargo no longer denies essential goods to Cuba. Several Latin American countries have resumed trade with Cuba. Spare parts for pre-1961 machines are still needed, but the major Cuban industries and its infrastructure are linked to products from socialist countries, Western Europe, and Japan. It might be less expensive to trade with the United States than with these other countries because of lower transporation costs. But with the powerful sugar and citrus lobbies that would operate if the embargo were lifted, Cuba would not be able to sell much to the United States and would probably try to avoid the imbalance likely to result from a one-way trading relationship. Thus Cuba has demanded an end to the embargo as a sign that the United States had abandoned the end for which the embargo was initiated: the destabilization and overthrow of the Cuban government.

Terrorism. When the United States ended its "secret" war against Cuba in 1963, it did not give up its secret army of exiles. Several continued to be paid by intelligence agencies, and others who had been trained and supported by the United States continued the war on their own.[24] In 1980 the Cuban exiles had organized training camps in the United States with Nicaraguan exiles. Although the Cuban exiles have focused their energy on overthrowing the Nicaraguan government, Cuba can hardly be certain that they will not attack Cuba again. Indeed, in recent years some exiles have penetrated into Cuba and destroyed facilities. Several Cuban exiles are members of an international terrorist network that has assassinated Cuban diplomats, bombed Cuban diplomatic missions, and blown up a Cuban commercial airliner. In 1978 the Federal Bureau of Investigation did share some information with Cuban authorities about the exile community. Cuba has asked that the United States again provide it with data to counter the terrorists and to cease any support for their activities.

Violation of Air Space. The United States began reconnaissance flights over Cuba in the summer of 1962 and triumphantly used photos from them in its UN presentation that condemned Soviet intrusion in the hemisphere. The flights continued for the next fifteen years, ostensibly to monitor Soviet compliance with the 1962 agreement on the removal of missiles. As a gesture of goodwill, President Carter canceled all reconnaissance flights over Cuba in 1977. But he reinstituted them in September 1979, after the "discovery" of the Soviet brigade, and they continue today. There is little practical purpose for the flights because of the U.S. satellite surveillance capability; therefore, they serve as no more than symbols of a hostile

U.S. posture. For Cuba they also represent an infringement on its sovereignty.

Guantanamo. The U.S. naval base on the southeast coast of Cuba poses only a minor threat to Cuban security and is an unreliable outpost for the United States, given its location. The United States has seized on the base's value as a symbol of the looming U.S. military might by holding occasional exercises from there.[25] To Cuba it is also a reminder of the hated 1901 Platt Amendment and the periods of U.S. occupation because it was forced to lease the base to the United States as a result of the amendment. Cuban insistence that the United States has no right to hold any of its land for a military base also rests on its concern about national sovereignty.

Stark Contrast

The contrast is stark between the positions of Cuba and the United States. None of Cuba's demands threatens fundamental security interests of the United States, and all are amenable to compromise. In contrast, the United States would have Cuba relinquish the security that the Soviet Union provides and renounce basic principles that are articulated in its constitution. Although there are some peripheral issues on which the two countries no doubt could have fruitful discussions, the U.S. stance precludes any meaningful negotiation on the question of normalizing relations. Without a change in the U.S. posture, then, there is little likelihood that there could be any movement toward a serious reduction in tension between the two countries.

Notes

1. This view was stated succinctly by Kenneth Skoug, head of the State Department's Office of Cuban Affairs: "U.S. policy toward Cuba is shaped primarily by our perception of Cuban conduct in international affairs." See Kenneth Skoug, "The United States and Cuba," U.S. State Department, Current Policy No. 646, December 17, 1984, p. 1. Also see Philip Brenner, "The Unchanging Agenda in U.S.-Cuban Relations," Paper presented at the Eleventh International Congress of the Latin American Studies Association, Mexico City, September 30, 1983, pp. 5–13.

2. John Ferch, "Cuban-American Relations: The U.S. Perspective," Paper presented at the International Roundtable: United States in the 1980s, Havana, Center for the Study of the Americas, March 16, 1983 (Spanish version), p. 6 (translation by author). At the time Ferch was chief of the U.S. Interests Section in Havana.

3. Skoug, "The United States and Cuba," pp. 2, 3.

4. Jim Hoagland, "Cuba Reconsiders 1962 Understanding," *Washington Post,* February 3, 1985, p. A25. Also, Alfonso Chardy, "Conservative Pressure Brings U.S. Review of '62 Accords on Cuba," *Miami Herald,* July 7, 1983, p. 12A.

5. Skoug, "The United States and Cuba," p. 3; *Report of the National Bipartisan Commission on Central America* [Kissinger Commission], January 1984, pp. 88–93; U.S. Departments of State and Defense, "The Soviet-Cuban Connection in Central America and the Caribbean," Washington, D.C., March 1985, pp. 3–10, 41.

6. This claim was validated by General Rafael del Pino, who defected from the Cuban air force in 1987. Though he was for the most part highly critical of the Cuban government, in an interview broadcast over Radio Marti he asserted that there are only 300 to 400 Cuban troops in Nicaragua. "Cuban Military Discontented, Defector Says," *Miami Herald,* June 30, 1987, p. 4A.

7. Bill Keller and Joel Brinkley, "U.S. Military Is Termed Prepared For Any Move Against Nicaragua," *New York Times,* June 4, 1985.

8. "Cuba Endorses Peace Plan for Central America," *Washington Post,* August 14, 1987, p. A18.

9. Wayne S. Smith, "Dateline Havana: Myopic Diplomacy," *Foreign Policy,* no. 48, Fall 1982, p. 170. Also see William M. LeoGrande, *Cuba's Policy in Africa, 1959–1980,* Policy Papers in International Affairs, no. 13 (Berkeley: University of California, 1980), pp. 13–22; Jorge I. Dominguez, "Cuban Foreign Policy," *Foreign Affairs,* vol. 57, no. 1, Fall 1978, pp. 96–97.

10. Jim Hoagland, "Castro Outlines Goals in Africa," *Washington Post,* February 6, 1985, p. A13; Alfonso Chardy, "Cuban: Pullout from Angola Is Unlikely Soon," *Miami Herald,* March 27, 1985, p. 18A.

11. Hoagland, "Castro Outlines Goals in Africa," p. A13.

12. "Fidel Castro's Closing Speech," Havana International Service, February 8, 1986, FBIS Daily Report Latin America, February 10, 1986, p. Q36.

13. Pamela S. Falk, "Cuba in Africa," *Foreign Affairs,* vol. 65, no. 5, Summer 1987, p. 1091.

14. Claire Robertson, "Angolan Proposal on Cuban Issue Studied," *Washington Post,* August 11, 1987, p. A21.

15. Falk, "Cuba in Africa," p. 1095.

16. Alfred L. Padula, Jr., "U.S. Business Squabbles Over Cuba," *Nation,* October 22, 1977, pp. 390–393.

17. Austin Linsley, "U.S.-Cuban Relations: The Role of Puerto Rico," in *Cuba in the World,* ed. Cole Blasier and Carmelo Mesa-Lago (Pittsburgh: University of Pittsburgh Press, 1979), pp. 122–123.

18. U.S. Senate, Committee on the Judiciary, "Terroristic Activity: The Cuban Connection in Puerto Rico; Castro's Hand in Puerto Rican and U.S. Terrorism: Hearings," 94th Cong., 1st Sess., July 30, 1975.

19. Wayne Smith, *The Closest of Enemies* (New York: Norton, 1987), p. 102.

20. Alfonso Chardy, "Reagan Officials Link Cubans, Sandinistas to Drug Trade," *Miami Herald,* August 3, 1984.

21. Peter Wyden, *Bay of Pigs: The Untold Story* (New York: Simon and Schuster, 1979), pp. 22–23.

22. Lewis Tambs, ed., "A New Inter-American Policy for the Eighties: Report of the Committee of Santa Fe" (Washington, D.C.: Council for Inter-American Security, 1981), p. 46.

23. Alfonso Chardy, "Despite Harsh Reply, U.S. Doubts Escalation," *Miami Herald,* May 21, 1985; Edward Cody, "Cuba Revises View of U.S.," *Washington Post,* June 5, 1985, p. A25.

24. John Dinges and Saul Landau, *Assassination on Embassy Row* (New York: Pantheon, 1980), pp. 246–251; Al Burt, "Miami Was Rife with Rumors of War," *Miami Herald,* December 11, 1983, p. 17M.

25. Max Azicri, "Cuba and the United States: What Happened to Rapprochement?" in *The New Cuban Presence in the Caribbean,* ed. Barry B. Levine (Boulder, Colo.: Westview, 1983), p. 178; Carla Anne Robbins, *The Cuban Threat* (New York: McGraw-Hill, 1983), p. 244.

CHAPTER 4

Factors Shaping
Cuba's Policy

IT IS SIGNIFICANT THAT CUBAN LEADERS now declare, for the first time, that they would be willing to negotiate the normalization of relations with the United States without any preconditions. This confidence reflects their assessment that Cuba today is strong enough to be flexible. There are also objective indicators of this strength.

Cuba has established a military capability that gives it protection from an invasion or an attempted overthrow of the regime. It also has achieved several developmental goals, and it has institutionalized the revolution. This strength and sense of security could enable Cuba—if the United States were interested in negotiations—to accommodate important U.S. interests.

Although current factors influence the particular direction of Cuban foreign policy today, the policy reflects two goals that have been maintained since 1959: to secure and to develop the revolution. Implementation of these objectives has been shaped by the nature of the threats against Cuba and by the nature of the world economy.

Of course, the primary threat to Cuban security remains a direct military attack by the United States. But the Cubans also understand that economic vulnerability has the potential to undermine the revolution; thus they see their security as entwined with their economic development. Their ability to achieve high health standards and literacy, to provide decent housing, and to meet basic nutritional requirements for the whole population strengthens the revolution, increases its legitimacy, and makes it less susceptible to attack. Yet this ability is compromised by Cuba's difficulty in obtaining hard currency and by indirect attacks, such as the U.S. economic embargo.

Even the very fear of attack stifles development because it leads Cuba to devote scarce resources to military preparedness.

These factors help to account for Cuba's relationship with the Soviet Union, a relationship that has preoccupied the United States. Without Soviet military assistance, Cuba would have been quite vulnerable to an invasion. Meanwhile, Soviet economic assistance has enabled Cuba to proceed with development plans while maintaining its military preparedness.

In a sense, then, Cuba's relations with both superpowers have influenced the course of the revolution. Yet, Cuba has maintained its own ideological perspective throughout: a vision of Third World solidarity, with an emphasis on socialist development.[1] Cuba emphasizes its ties both to Africa—much of its population descends from slaves originating in Africa—and to Latin America. Cuban soldiers have died in combat in both Africa and Latin America, and Cuba supports aid programs throughout both regions.

Internationalism in Cuba's foreign policy has taken many forms, including the support of guerrillas attempting to overthrow governments in Latin America; the deployment of troops in defense of governments in Africa; and the pursuit of Third World diplomatic initiatives through the nonaligned movement. Some of these activities have incurred significant costs and have weakened Cuba's pursuit of security and development. Cuba's activities in Latin America during the early 1960s, for example, led the Organization of American States to suspend Cuba's membership and endorse the U.S. embargo.

Yet, Cuba perceives internationalism to be a framework that ultimately serves its two goals. If it can diversify its dependency, which would mean relying on Third World as well as industrialized nations, it is less likely to be submerged by the interests of either superpower. Furthermore, as a small country, it expects that it is more likely to find succor from other small countries with similar developmental perspectives than from advanced industrialized nations.

This ideology does not guide Cuba with a rigid, dogmatic set of formulas. Indeed, a hallmark of the Cuban revolution is its pragmatism in pursuit of security and development. For example, Cuba maintained good relations with Spain under the Franco dictatorship because Franco did not participate in the U.S. embargo. In Latin America, with the rise of left-leaning governments during the 1970s, Cuba largely abandoned its support of guerrillas and emphasized state-to-state relations.

The way these factors combine to influence Cuban foreign policy can be seen from a review of key decisions taken at the Third

Congress of the Cuban Communist Party, which was held in February and December, 1986. The party congress focused on problems of economic efficiency and linked this concern to its affirmation of a decision to integrate Cuba more fully into the socialist economic bloc, the Council for Mutual Economic Assistance (CMEA). It also approved plans to restructure Cuba's defense forces and simultaneously diminished the military's power within the Communist party. Finally, it reaffirmed existing commitments in Latin America and Africa.

Setting of the Party Congress

Successes

Though the Communist party has been the governing organization in Cuba since 1965, it did not become closely linked to the Communist parties in other countries until the 1970s. Fidel Castro's July 26th Movement effectively controlled the government after the 1959 revolution, and through a series of reorganizations, the movement absorbed members of the Popular Socialist (Communist) party and other radical organizations. When the July 26th Movement leaders declared this new party—which aggregated many of the earlier radical factions—to be the official Communist party of Cuba in 1965, it bore little resemblance to the party that had been close to the Soviet Union before 1959. Its first congress was held only in 1975.[2]

The party congress is the main policymaking assembly of the Cuban Communist party. Made up of delegates from party units throughout the country, the congress serves to assess how well the political and economic goals established at the prior congress were met. It also sets new goals for the next five years, affirms decisions about the restructuring of key organizations, and establishes the guidelines for party members to follow.

The third party congress met at a time when Cuban leaders were feeling that the revolution had achieved a significant measure of security and had made major developmental gains. They saw Cuba's foreign policy as serving the revolution's interests quite well. In Latin America, for example, from 1982 to 1986 they had witnessed a turnaround from the deteriorating relations of the prior three years.[3] The change started with the 1982 Malvinas/Falklands War (the conflict between Great Britain and Argentina over control of Malvinas/Falklands Islands, which lie off the Argentine coast), during which Cuba offered to provide military assistance to Argentina. By 1985, Argentina had surpassed Mexico as Cuba's largest trading partner in the region and was supplying it with millions of dollars in new credits.[4] The emergence of new democracies also fueled the trend to warmer relations. Brazil, Uruguay, and Bolivia began to reestablish diplomatic and commercial contacts in 1984. In 1987, Cuba had full diplomatic relations with fifteen countries in the hemisphere, including Canada and Mexico, and varying degrees of relations with ten others.

Although Cuba's poverty and heavy dependence on the sale of sugar as a source of hard currency indicated that it still had much to develop, by the 1986 congress there had been significant internal development and less need to import basic goods. Sugarcane was being harvested by machines built in Cuba, and this freed workers for other productive activities. There were notable advances in high technology: A genetic engineering facility was expected to rival similar enterprises in the United States and Europe; silicon chips were being produced for a domestic computer industry; a new hospital center in Havana was using state-of-the-art equipment for advanced medical research and sophisticated treatment. Consumer goods were more readily available, and stores were stocked with an increasing variety of products.[5]

Moreover, the revolution had achieved several basic developmental goals, and the effects of development had been felt fairly equally by all segments of the population. Illiteracy had been nearly eradicated. Caloric intake exceeded the prerevolutionary level. Life expectancy had been extended to seventy-four years. The widely acclaimed health care system had reduced the level of infant mortality to 16.5 deaths per 1,000 live births (a year later it was 13). The cities had not become swollen with the sorts of shanties that dot the outskirts of most Latin American urban centers, because the focus of much of the development in Cuba had been in rural areas.

A perception that the revolution was strong accounts, in part, for two potentially important changes that occurred around the time of the party congress. Cuba released a large number of political prisoners in 1985 and 1986.[6] Officials spoke about their intention to free all inmates imprisoned for political crimes.[7] In addition, the officials began to develop a new relationship with the Catholic church and with Protestant denominations. In February 1986, almost 200 Catholic bishops, clergy, and lay people held an unprecedented conference in Havana to discuss Christian life in Cuba.[8] This followed the publication of a series of conversations between a Brazilian friar and Fidel Castro, in which the Cuban leader asserted that Christianity could be reconciled with Marxism.[9] The Communist party also designated a member of the central committee to be responsible for religious life, which was a significant acknowledgment by the party of the legitimacy of religion.

Problems

Based on these circumstances, the Cuban leaders were confident, but they did not dwell on successes at the party congress. Instead, the leaders emphasized problems in the economy. Moreover, between the February and December sessions of the congress, Castro began a "rectification" process in which he called on Cubans to work harder, to be willing to sacrifice personal (consumer) desires, and to value collective interests rather than personal gain.[10] The Cuban government also closed the private farmers' markets that had been created in the early 1980s.[11]

There is little doubt that the Cuban economy has encountered serious problems.[12] Whereas the gross social product grew at an impressive 7.3 percent average annual rate from 1980 to 1984, the rate in 1985 was 4.8 percent. Cuba's balance-of-payments deficit with the West has been $500 million annually, and it owes Western banks $3.5 billion.[13] Yet Cuba compares favorably to other countries in the region. No other country experienced so high a rate of growth, and in the same period the average gross domestic product for Latin America as a whole was virtually unchanged. Latin American external debt is nearly $400 billion.[14]

Certainly, the stability of Cuba's growth can be attributed in part to the special relationship Cuba enjoys with the Soviet Union. By some accounts, Soviet price subsidies on Cuba's export of sugar and import of oil, along with direct economic assistance, amount to what may be more than $4 billion annually.[15] While Cuba suffered along with other sugar-producing countries in Latin America when the world price dropped below four cents, it was reselling perhaps as much as two-thirds of its Soviet oil shipments for a handsome profit. More than a third of Cuba's internationally convertible (hard) currency earnings derive from the sale of oil.[16]

Here, however, lay one source of its economic worries. As the price of oil on the international market dropped, Cuba needed to increase its export of other goods to the West in order to obtain hard currency. Trade with capitalist countries had declined from a high of 40.5 percent of all Cuban trade in 1975 to 15 percent in 1985. This problem required immediate attention and thus dominated the third party congress.

Increasing Ties to the Socialist Bloc

Economic Ties

Cuba has been trading with the Eastern European socialist countries since 1960, but until the 1980s it had not coordinated its own economic plans fully with those of the CMEA countries. Once it did so, Cuba needed to improve its reliability as a supplier: Inefficiency had weakened Cuba's ability to meet production targets. Full integration into the CMEA meant that Cuba would plan its economy in accord with the socialist nations. Although this deprives Cuba of some autonomy, the country can reasonably expect that its basic economic needs will be met in the foreseeable future. This is a situation in which few if any Third World countries find themselves, and it undoubtedly contributes enormously to Cuba's sense of security.

Yet, the CMEA countries do not satisfy all of Cuba's needs, with the result that Cuba also seeks to import some goods from the West, for which it needs hard currency. Thus efficiency also was associated with the goal of enabling Cuba to export more to the West, in order to earn hard currency, and of increasing the rate of import substitution, to decrease the need for imports.

The decision to tie Cuba into the CMEA network even more tightly was announced by Castro in his main report to the party congress: "Our socialist economic integration within the framework of the CMEA will be increased. Priority will be given to developing the machine and electronics industry, light industry, pharmaceuticals, biotechnology, and sugar-cane by-products as important areas that will generate new exports. . . . Agricultural development will be stepped up . . . contributing to more exports of traditional agricultural products."[17] In effect, the economic plan outline envisioned a development strategy of import substitution, under which Cuba would produce its own foodstuffs, clothing, and small appliances. It also would moderately expand exports to Western countries, in order to depend less on the Soviet Union for hard currency. Most significantly, the plan calls for Cuba to remain a raw materials supplier nation under an international socialist division of labor. It would be expected to increase its sugar, citrus, tobacco, and nickel deliveries to CMEA countries, and to do so on a well-regulated schedule.

Political Ties

Cuba's relationship with the Soviet Union brought it into the socialist economic bloc. This new set of international trading partners replaced those that had vanished when U.S.-led Western nations closed their markets. As with any ties, the links to the East have had particular effects on Cuban development. Cuba is dependent on imports for several essential goods, such as oil; therefore, it must be able to produce goods that in effect are used in exchange for the imports. Thus, like most small countries, Cuba's market affects its economic decisions. In its case, choices about which goods to produce are dominated by the "demand" of the socialist countries because most of Cuba's foreign trade occurs with them. Close contact with the Eastern bloc countries also has led Cuba to borrow economic models from them. Finally, and not surprisingly, because of the importance of these ties to Cuban security and development, Cuba also has constrained its international behavior at times to conform to the interests of the Soviet Union.

It would be reasonable to expect that with even closer economic ties to the Soviet trading bloc, there will be some added Soviet influence on Cuban policies. Yet past practice suggests that Cuban foreign policy will not be a slave to Soviet whim. As veteran diplomat Wayne Smith observed, Cuba "has its own interests and objectives—which may differ markedly from those of the Soviet Union—and within the parameters defined by its relationship with Moscow, it pursues its own agenda in its own way."[18] At times, Cuba's agenda may seem to parallel the Soviet Union's. Yet it would be salutary for the United States to distinguish between the policies of the two countries. Cuba's primary concern is its own security needs, and it has the capacity to respond independently to the United States. Where U.S. and Cuban interests conflict directly, there is room for the United States to pursue its interests without involving the Soviet Union.

To be sure, Cuba has acted against some of its own interests at the behest of its patron. Most prominently, when Cuba refused to condemn the 1979 Soviet invasion of Afghanistan, it lost credibility as a leader of the nonaligned countries, especially because Fidel Castro was president of the movement at the time. But the notion that Cuba is a "proxy" state for the Soviet Union has been discredited by evidence of significant differences between the two countries.[19] In Angola, for example, Cuba differed with the Soviet Union over the backing of a threatened coup against President Agostinho Neto. In Ethiopia, although Cuban troops fought under the Soviet Union's general command, the two countries differed over military involvement against the Eritrean rebels.[20]

The relationship between Cuba and the Soviet Union is best characterized as two sovereign countries with compatible and often complementary interests. One indication of this is that Cuba has influenced Soviet foreign policy. It seems clear, now, that the Cubans convinced the Soviets to provide full support for the MPLA in Angola after Cuba had made its own commitments.[21] In Grenada, from 1979 to 1983, Cuba appears to have acted as a "broker" for the Grenadians, trying to secure assistance from a reticent Soviet Union.[22]

A continuing Cuban concern about the Soviet Union is the still ambiguous commitment to defend Cuba. Political scientist Michael Erisman observed that "as long as Moscow refuses to give Cuba an open, ironclad guarantee that it will respond to any U.S. attack on the island with whatever protective counterforce is necessary, the Fidelistas can never feel truly safe."[23] Of course, the Soviet Union has provided Cuba with enormous military capabilities, including several versions of the MIG-23, the best Soviet tanks, surface-to-air missiles, and an assortment of arms. From 1981 to 1985, moreover, the Soviet Union doubled the average annual tonnage of military equipment it sent to Cuba.[24] However, the logistics of defending Cuba over a long distance, the reasonable Cuban skepticism about Soviet willingness to risk a wider war in the event of an attack, and the lack of an overt promise make Cuban leaders wary about relying wholly on Soviet defenses. Their worry, in part, led to changes in the structure of the Cuban military forces over the past five years, which were reflected in decisions at the party congress.

Strengthening Internal Structures: Party and Military

Party

A hint that the third party congress might ratify important changes within the party came in mid-1985, when several high party officials lost their ministerial posts. The list included the powerful minister of interior, who had responsibility for the national police and intelligence service. It also contained the ministers of public health, transportation, and light industry, and the presidents of the sports institute, radio and television institute, and Academy of Science. The first three ministers also had been on the Communist party's fourteen-member political bureau—its most powerful organ—and the congress removed them from this elite body as well.

Party leaders wanted to signal to a new generation that the system was not closed, that there was room for both mobility and disagreement. They seem to have been concerned about the basis of the party's legitimacy, which had rested for twenty-seven years on the revolutionary credentials of the leaders. Power had been held by a small circle of people who claimed the right to rule because of their involvement in the war against Batista and in the establishment of the current regime. Repeatedly there had been talk of the need for "socialismo sin sociolismo," that is, socialism based on firmer ground than an old boy network or personal relations. The most dramatic decision in this regard was the dismissal of Ramiro Valdes Menendez, the interior minister, who had been one of the founding fathers of the revolution in 1953.[25] His generation was reaching the age when it had to consider the transition to a new form of legitimacy for Cuba's next set of rulers. The transition, in Max Weber's terms, is one of moving from authority that rests on a "personal *gift of grace*" to one based on rational/legal rules.[26]

One criterion for rationality appears to be a type of quota. The Communist party has 523,000 members. Efforts were made to increase the proportion of women, nonwhites, and younger members in the party and in the new leadership. Thus the governing central committee now has nearly the same percentage of women as the whole party, though the proportion of women in the party rose in five years from only 18.8 to 21.5 percent.[27] In part, Cuban leaders were influenced by their 1980 critique of the Polish Communist party, which they believed was not responsive to its mass base.[28] They allege that efforts were made, therefore, to increase the number of people on the central committee from occupations previously underrepresented. In fact, the representation of workers and farmers did increase marginally. Most significantly, though, the process increased the power of the Communist party itself, because the greatest proportional increase came from new central committee members whose work was in the party bureaucracy.

The dismissal of Valdes signaled also the intention of some Communist party leaders to improve the human rights atmosphere in Cuba. During the first of Valdes's two periods of control over the intelligence, police, and domestic security forces, there allegedly had been numerous human rights abuses. He was seen as a hardliner, and according to some Cuban government sources, he had been brought back to the interior ministry in 1980 after the Mariel exodus in order to "contain" popular discontent. He was replaced by his deputy, General José Abrantes Fernandez, whose human rights credentials are unclear, but whose personal authority to violate the law would be quite inferior to that of Valdes.[29]

To be sure, judgments about the opening of the Cuban system cannot be made merely on the basis of demotions that may be no more than symbolic, regardless of how deeply the ousted officials had been involved in the development of Cuban politics. Still, their departures change the internal dynamics of the Communist party and create opportunity for further change.

Military

The tradition of Cuban military involvement in the running of government dates back nearly to the start of the century. Since 1959 the Revolutionary Armed Forces (FAR) has been the most powerful organization in Cuba next to the Communist party. The leaders of the guerrilla army, which the FAR replaced, became the leaders of the present regime. As in the guerrilla army, responsibilities often have overlapped between the military and civilian sectors. The link between the two sectors was personal, as particular people had dual roles, in a pattern that Jorge Dominguez characterized as that of the "civic-soldier."[30]

In light of its power and prominence, therefore, the reduction in FAR representation from 50 to 34 members on the 225-person central committee is striking. At the end of the second party congress, 27 percent of the central committee were military officers; now it is 15 percent.[31] Not only does the loss of representation diminish immediately the military's power within this major policymaking body, but also the decision deprives the military of the aura of being the easiest route to power for subsequent generations and thereby reduces the military's influence at all levels of the society.

The official explanation for the reduction focused on the party's efforts to increase the proportion of members from underrepresented sectors while it held the size of the central committee constant. But this rationale begs the question of why the military bore such a large brunt of the redistribution, or why maintaining a fixed central committee size took precedence over retaining FAR influence on the committee.

A more likely explanation is that the FAR lost power in the central committee because the party sought to reduce the military's role in national security and in civilian affairs. With resistance likely to come from the military because of its diminished authority, the party undoubtedly needed to undermine the FAR's representation in order to effect its decision.

Indeed, it took extraordinary leverage for the party to develop a new institution—Territorial Troop Militias (MTT)—which now shares the FAR's essential responsibility for defending the island. At the congress, the party ratified a new mode of territorial defense, characterized as a "people in arms." It pictures an invasion by the United States that would be countered by protracted warfare from citizen-guerrillas. The principal task of the regular army would be merely to provide sufficient time for the militia to mobilize. There are now 1.5 million members of the MTT. It has light infantry weapons and combat equipment, receives periodic training, and accounts for an increasing portion of the military budget.[32]

President Castro described the military change to editors of the *Washington Post* in 1985. "Before," he said, "war was the job of the army and the reserves, while the rest of the citizens did nothing more than watch what went on; today, it is the concern of every citizen."[33] He now heads an informal Council of Defense, accountable to the party, which would run military operations in the event of an attack.

The events in Grenada confirmed a decision made in 1981: to abandon sole reliance on the FAR for Cuba's defense and to complement it with the MTT. Although the FAR had garnered respect for its Angola and Ethiopian operations, there was condemnation of the military's inaction during the 1983 U.S. invasion of Grenada. Ragtag Cuban construction workers, not the polished military advisers who were in Grenada, held the U.S. marines at bay. The advisers surrendered quickly, and the officers in charge were disgraced upon their return to Cuba.

The 1981 decision to create the MTT was made because the Cubans believed that a U.S. invasion was a real possibility during the Reagan administration.[34] Moreover, a feeble Soviet leadership obsessed with the Polish crisis (following the Polish government's suppression of the Solidarity trade union movement in 1980) was not a source of strength on which the Cubans felt they could rely. Thus in 1981 Cuba requested increased arms from the Soviet Union for the MTT, and this flow of arms accounts in part for the growth in shipments since then.[35] The Grenada invasion led Cuba to speed up development of the militia because the invasion enhanced fears that the military had grown complacent and that the FAR's concept of defense might not serve to deter an invasion at home.

Cuba has now developed what might be called the "Swiss" form of deterrence against invasion.[36] Were any country even to contemplate an attack, it would need to consider that the Cubans could have on their beaches a force of armed people larger than any likely landing party.

The Strength to Be Flexible

Writing in 1978, Jorge Dominguez observed that "the survival of revolutionary rule remains the foremost objective of their [Cuban] foreign policy."[37] Nothing has happened since then to contradict his conclusion, and the third party congress only adds further evidence to buttress it. Increased Cuban integration in the CMEA and the restructuring of the military are actions that reflect a search for security. It would be reasonable to associate Cuba's move toward the Eastern bloc in the mid-1980s with the increased threat posed by the United States during that time.

Although Cuba views the United States with apprehension, it also has the capacity now to be flexible with respect to the United States. It has achieved many developmental goals, especially with respect to health and education, and has less to fear in opening up to the United States. Its ties to the Soviet Union, while providing an imperfect security umbrella, continue to give Cuba the wherewithal to deter an invasion and to maintain steady economic growth. Replacement of the second tier of the Communist party's leadership and reforming the role of the military give Cuba a sense that the revolution has been institutionalized and will endure. Cuba's renewed links to Latin America and outreach to the Catholic church reflect a dynamism and pragmatism that could be applied to efforts at normalizing relations with the United States.

Cuba recognizes that as a developing country it cannot be economically independent. But when world economic conditions in the mid-1970s gave it some freedom to choose, Cuba opted to diversify its dependency between East and West. It has generally defined its security in terms of not being dependent on a sole source of sustenance. This perspective is evident in Cuba's internationalist solidarity, against which the United States rails. Cuba apparently hopes to create a bloc of Third World nations that might be willing and able to sustain each other apart from the developed countries. Such a circumstance would not be necessarily antagonistic to U.S. interests. Indeed, there is not a predetermined incompatibility between U.S. interests and Cuban national security. U.S. interests could be partly satisfied by diminishing, rather than intensifying, Cuba's concern for its security.

Notes

1. See Carlos Rafael Rodriguez, "Strategic Foundations of Cuban Foreign Policy," in *The Cuba Reader,* ed. Philip Brenner, William M. LeoGrande, Donna Rich, and Daniel Siegel (New York: Grove, forthcoming).

2. Jorge I. Dominguez, *Cuba: Order and Revolution* (Cambridge: Harvard University Press, 1978), pp. 210–218; William M. LeoGrande, "Party Development in Revolutionary Cuba," in *The Cuba Reader,* ed. Philip Brenner, et al.

3. While it sought to be a leader and champion of Latin America, Cuba also became a pariah in the 1960s for its support of revolutionary movements. In the 1970s, however, Cuba emphasized the importance of state-to-state relations, as conditions in the hemisphere changed. By 1975 the Organization of American States voted to lift its embargo against Cuba and permitted countries to renew economic and political relations. This warming trend was disrupted at the start of the 1980s by four factors. First, Cuba's refusal to condemn the Soviet invasion of Afghanistan resurrected some ill will, especially among Latin American members of the Non-Aligned Movement. Second, Cuba antagonized Peru and Venezuela in its handling of embassy incidents that led to the 1980 Mariel exodus. Relations with Venezuela already had been tense because of Venezuela's refusal to expedite prosecution of three terrorists involved in the 1976 bombing of a Cuban airliner, an act that killed seventy-three people. Third, the election of conservative governments in countries where Cuba had begun to establish good relations—such as Colombia, Costa Rica, Jamaica, and Saint Lucia—reversed these movements. Finally, the Reagan administration made strong efforts to isolate Cuba.

4. William R. Long, "Cuba, Latin America's Black Sheep, Is Gaining in Effort to Get Back Into the Fold," *Los Angeles Times,* August 8, 1986, p. 10. See also Mimi Whitefield, "New Latin Democracies Warm to Cuba," *Miami Herald,* March 23, 1985, p. 1A; Boris Yopo H., "El reacercamiento de Cuba con America Latina," *Cono Sur* (Santiago de Chile), January-March 1986, pp. 9–11.

5. Sam Dillon, "Cuba's Economy Shifts Its Focus," *Miami Herald,* February 10, 1986, p. 4A.

6. Lourdes Meluza, "Cuba Reportedly Frees 47 Political Prisoners," *Miami Herald,* July 10, 1986, p. 9A. In a symbolic gesture, Cuba released the one remaining imprisoned senior officer of the Bay of Pigs invasion in June 1986. See Julia Preston, "Cuba to Free Last Jailed Bay of Pigs Commander," *Washington Post,* June 8, 1986, p. A21. Also see Joseph B. Treaster, "Cuba and Human Rights: 2 Versions," *New York Times,* May 21, 1987, p. A3.

7. The number of people classified as "political prisoners" varies widely. The U.S. Catholic Conference in 1986 listed nearly 1,000 people as political prisoners. (See Sandra Dibble, "Castro Says He'll Let 348 Leave Cuba," *Miami Herald,* June 9, 1987, p. 1.) In interviews with the author in 1987, Cuban officials claimed to have fewer than 400 incarcerated, after releasing the 348. This contrasts with the several thousand they acknowledged in the late 1970s, when the Carter administration successfully negotiated the issue with the Castro government. In 1987, Freedom House, an anticommunist research group, alleged that there were still several thousand political prisoners. One reason for the differences may turn on the definition of political prisoner. In an interview with the author on July 13, 1987, Fidel Castro asserted that no person had ever been imprisoned for his or her beliefs. He said that a person is classified as a political prisoner for an action he or she takes, such as sabotage, espionage, or bombing, that has

a political intent. An alternative perspective is offered by former political prisoner Armando Valladares in his controversial book, *Against All Hope,* trans. Andrew Hurley (New York: Knopf, 1985). Cuban officials note that Valladares had been a member of the Batista police in 1959 and was arrested for urban bombings, not for his poetry (which was nonexistent before his arrest).

8. Sam Dillon, "In Exchange for Freedom to Exist, Church Gives Cuba a Tacit Blessing," *Miami Herald,* February 23, 1986, p. 9A. Also see Margaret Crahan, "Freedom of Worship in Revolutionary Cuba," in *The Cuba Reader,* ed. Brenner et al.

9. *Fidel y La Religion: Conversaciones con Frei Betto* (Havana: Oficina de Publicaciones del Consejo de Estado, 1985), pp. 324–326.

10. In his closing speech to the third party congress, Castro focused on economic problems and the need for renewal, which he described as a process of "rectification." He declared—and the party newspaper featured his statement—that "a revolutionary consciousness, communist spirit, sense of mission, and will has been, is, and will always be a thousand times more powerful than money." See *Granma,* December 5, 1987 (daily Spanish edition, translation by the author). Also see "Castro Warns of Hardships," *Miami Herald,* December 4, 1986, p. 1A.

11. Sam Dillon, "Castro Attacks 'Neocapitalists,' Corrupt Workers," *Miami Herald,* July 26, 1986, p. 1A. In an interview with the author in July 1987, Vice President Carlos Rafael Rodriguez asserted that these markets, open in various forms since 1980, had produced gains largely for middlemen and not for farmers and had accounted for only one-ninth of the sales of the "parallel markets." The latter are state run and buy excess produce from small farmers for sale at prices higher than regular state-run stores. Perhaps of greater significance, the private markets disrupted agricultural production because farmers would steal and borrow state equipment to harvest and transport their produce for the private market.

12. Roger Lowenstein, "Castro Looks to West For Help in Bolstering Sick Cuban Economy," *Wall Street Journal,* June 18, 1985, p. 1; Alfonso Chardy, "For Cuban Economy, '85 Was a Very Bad Year," *Miami Herald,* January 26, 1986, p. 30A.

13. Juan del Aguila, "Political Developments in Cuba," *Current History,* January 1986, pp. 12–13; Chardy, "For Cuban Economy, '85 Was a Very Bad Year"; "Main Report, Third Party Congress," *Granma Weekly Review,* February 16, 1986, p. 2. The gross social product is a measure of goods and services produced in Cuba, and is roughly equivalent to the gross domestic product measurement used in capitalist countries.

14. James L. Rowe, Jr., "The Latin American Debt Morass," *Washington Post,* August 16, 1987, p. H1; Andres Oppenheimer, "Latin Exports to Show 9% Decline," *Miami Herald,* Business Monday section, December 16, 1985, p. 24; Inter-American Development Bank, *Economic and Social Progress in Latin America: 1985 Report* (Washington: Inter-American Development Bank, 1985), p. 388.

15. Pamela Falk, *Cuban Foreign Policy* (Lexington, Mass.: D. C. Heath, 1985), p. 136. The measurement of this subsidy is much in dispute among economists and depends on calculations of what the Soviet Union and Cuba might obtain, respectively, for their products on the international market. For example, if the typically high "spot" market price for oil is used as a basis for calculating how much less Cuba pays for oil from the Soviet Union than it would pay otherwise, the subsidy would appear larger than if lower, long-term contract prices are used.

16. Rosalind Resnick, "Cuba Besieged," *Miami Herald,* March 29, 1987, p. C1; Jose de Cordoba, "Nose Dive in World Oil Prices Puts Cuba Economy over Barrel," *Miami Herald,* April 12, 1986, p. 12A. Also, interview with Cuban official, 1986; Falk, *Cuban Foreign Policy,* p. 136.

17. "Main Report, Third Party Congress," p. 9. Castro also exclaimed (p. 8): "Equal importance is attached to ensuring our country's contribution to the Comprehensive Plan for Scientific and Technological Development up to the year 2000 recently adopted by the CMEA." Also see *Programa del Partido Comunista de Cuba* (La Habana: Editora Politica, 1987), p. 27.

18. Wayne S. Smith, "The Cuba-Soviet Alliance," paper prepared for Johns Hopkins University-DISEU Conference, March 19–23, 1986, Havana, Cuba, p. 2. Similarly, Mark Katz contends, "Soviet and Cuban foreign policies have since the late 1960s served mainly to support each other." See "The Soviet-Cuban Connection," *International Security,* Summer 1983, p. 101. Also see Robert Pastor, "Cuba and the Soviet Union: Does Cuba Act Alone?" in *The New Cuban Presence in the Caribbean,* ed. Barry B. Levine (Boulder, Colo.: Westview, 1983).

19. William M. LeoGrande, "Cuba," in *Confronting Revolution,* ed. Morris J. Blachman, William M. LeoGrande, and Kenneth Sharpe (New York: Pantheon, 1986), pp. 250–252.

20. William M. LeoGrande, *Cuba's Policy in Africa, 1959–1980,* Policy Papers in International Affairs, no. 13 (Berkeley: University of California, 1980), pp. 25, 42–44.

21. Ibid., pp. 15–25; Katz, "The Soviet-Cuban Connection," pp. 94–96; Jorge Dominguez, "Cuban Foreign Policy," *Foreign Affairs,* Fall 1978, pp. 96–97.

22. Lourdes Meluza, "Cuba was 'Broker' for Grenada in Soviet Dealings, Scholar Says," *Miami Herald,* August 19, 1985, p. 1B.

23. H. Michael Erisman, *Cuba's International Relations* (Boulder, Colo.: Westview, 1985), p. 175. Also see Katz, "The Soviet-Cuban Connection," p. 105.

24. Phyllis Greene Walker, "National Security," in *Cuba: A Country Study,* ed. James Rudolph, U.S. Army Foreign Area Studies Handbook Series (Washington: Government Printing Office, 1987), pp. 261–262; Katz, "The Soviet-Cuban Connection," pp. 107–108.

25. A similar message was sent by the removal of hard-line central committee ideologist Antonio Perez Herrero. See Lourdes Meluza, "Castro Has Purged Nine Top Officials, Experts Say," *Miami Herald,* July 23, 1985, p. 9A.

26. Max Weber, "Politics as a Vocation," in *From Max Weber,* ed. H. H. Gerth and C. Wright Mills (New York: Oxford University Press, 1958), p. 79.

27. See Fidel Castro, *Informe Central [Main Report]: Tercer Congreso del Partido Comunista de Cuba* (Havana: Editora Politica, 1986), p. 92.

28. *Main Report: Second Congress of the Communist Party of Cuba,* reprinted in *Cuba Update* (Center for Cuban Studies), March 1981, p. 38.

29. In May 1986, the U.S. State Department released a study, "Human Rights in Castro's Cuba," which charged that Cuba fails to meet acceptable standards in every human rights category. However, specific charges were not verified in the manner of international human rights organizations, and many were based on old congressional testimony and anecdotes. Cuba has not permitted any official human rights group to monitor its internal actions. Yet impressionistic evidence, based on visits by officials from such groups, indicates that there is not a pattern of gross and systematic human rights violations.

30. Jorge Dominguez, *Cuba: Order and Revolution* (Cambridge: Harvard University Press, 1978), pp. 308–313. Also see Walker, "National Security," pp. 246–248.

31. In the 1980s their number actually increased to over 30 percent of the central committee: Walker, "National Security," p. 247. In what was undoubtedly an attempt to console the FAR, General Abelardo Colome Ibarra was promoted to full member status on the political bureau.

32. Aguila, "Political Developments in Cuba," pp. 14–15; "Main Report," *Granma Weekly Review,* February 16, 1986, p. 10.

33. "Entrevista con los periodistas del Washington Post," *Granma,* February 11, 1985, as quoted in Ramonet, "Cuba: Renovation dans la Revolution?" p. 3 (author's translation).

34. Walker, "National Security," p. 252.

35. Ramonet, "Cuba: Renovation dans la Revolution?" p. 2; also, interviews with Cuban officials, 1986, in Walker, "National Security," p. 261.

36. George Kennan provides an interesting theoretical discussion of this notion of deterrence, though without reference to Cuba, in "A New Philosophy of Defense," *New York Review of Books,* February 13, 1986, pp. 3–6.

37. Dominguez, "Cuban Foreign Policy," p. 84.

CHAPTER 5

Domestic Factors Shaping U.S. Policy

THOUGH A CASUAL OBSERVER might think that the obstacles to a change in U.S. policy toward Cuba are enormous, a review of the domestic politics that affect this policy indicates that there is greater room for movement than might be anticipated. Outside of the executive branch of the government, the combination of voices supporting and opposing a policy change generates an equivocal message. Neither side has a preponderance of force, and among the opponents of normalization there are substantial differences. As a result, the executive is relatively free to shape the policy. An administration that sought to reduce tension between Cuba and the United States would not necessarily be constrained in a significant way by domestic political factors. Yet it could not count on much support either. Let us consider how these forces are arrayed in each of the following areas: among interest groups, in the Congress, and in the press and public at large.

Interest Groups

Over the past twenty-five years, groups adamantly opposed to the normalization of relations between the United States and Cuba have seemed single-minded and have been the most vociferous. This has led commentators to believe that the opposition to normalization is monolithic and that there are virtually no forces in support of normal relations. Neither belief has validity. There are a variety of policies that could satisfy the interests of those who have opposed relations, and groups that support normalization represent considerable bases of power.

Opponents of Change

Until 1982, the Cuban Nationalist Movement and Brigade 2506 were the most prominent organizations opposed to relations between the United States and Cuba. They worked outside of traditional political forums and allegedly had links to terrorist organizations. By the early 1980s, a growing number of Cuban-American business leaders and elected officials had begun to disavow them.[1] Several of them have turned to the Cuban-American National Foundation (CANF), which was organized in 1981 and quickly spawned a Washington lobbying unit. It, too, has advocated an undeviating hard line against any relations with Cuba, and its political action committee has supported conservative, principally Republican candidates.[2] In May 1985, the CANF was rewarded for its determined support of President Reagan by his presence at one of the organization's fund-raisers in Miami.

Although the CANF is nominally nonpartisan, its close links to the Republican party diminish its ability to lead groups with multiple interests that require a good rapport with Democrats in Congress. Its partisan character also would weaken its influence with a Democratic administration.[3] Moreover the inflexibility of the CANF has the potential of undermining its own base of support. For example, its lobbying for Radio Marti may have won it plaudits from President Reagan and initially from Miami Cubans. But the loss of visiting privileges for exiles, which was Cuba's form of retaliation against the station, may rebound against CANF. Even among exiles who strongly oppose relations with Cuba, the program of visits had been popular.[4]

Less extreme, and less significant, are those opponents of change with outstanding monetary claims against Cuba. Some of the large claimants are represented by the Joint Corporate Committee on Cuban Claims (JCCCC), which has demanded that Cuba reimburse former owners for expropriated property before the United States begins any process of normalization. However, a majority of the large claimants do not support the JCCCC. Some, such as Coca-Cola and General Motors, expect that future business with Cuba will provide compensation enough.[5] Several have written off the loss and received generous tax deductions on the basis of inflated values. A few have sold their claims to speculators who paid as little as five cents on the dollar for a claim. Others may recognize that the most likely route to compensation would be less hostility toward Cuba, as Cuba has compensated property owners from countries with which it has normal relations.

Citrus and sugar companies support the U.S. embargo from fear of competition with Cuban produce. Cuba has approximately 60 percent as much acreage under citrus production as does Florida. U.S. cane and beet sugar interests already suffer from inroads made by corn and artificial sweeteners, and they actively protect themselves from all foreign competitors. In 1977 they were successful in thwarting even modest attempts by some members of Congress to relax the embargo. But the narrowness of their interest makes it susceptible to satisfaction—through special trade restrictions and price supports—that fall far short of an embargo.

Although groups opposed to normalization thus present an obstacle to a change in U.S. policy, their interests do not lead inexorably to a position of hostility because lessened tension need not conflict with the interests of all the groups. Their significance is often overestimated only because the groups that favor a relaxation in tension are so much weaker.

Proponents of Change

It has often been said, and it remains true, that there is virtually no natural domestic constituency for a normalization of relations with Cuba. Still, in contrast to opponents of normalization, the interests of the various groups that call for normal relations are compatible. Though they differ about the timing of normalization, they agree that it should be the end of a process that could start with accords on lesser issues. Their weakness derives in part from their small number and also from the lack of intensity in several of the groups.

On one end, there are Cuban-Americans who have advocated a resumption of normal relations between Cuba and the United States as soon as possible.[6] They reflect the generational dynamics within the Cuban-American community. Older members of the community, who chose to leave the island when they were adults, tend to be strongly anti-Castro. Their children, however, range across the political spectrum.[7] Many want to visit their "homeland" and to reestablish ties with families there.

The most prominent organization that represents Cuban-Americans who favor a change in policy is the Cuban-American Committee. It has a small office in Washington and maintains close contact with non-Cuban Hispanic groups. In the late 1970s, several of its supporters spearheaded the effort—through the Committee of 75—to open a "dialogue" with Cuba. One result of the dialogue was the decision by the Cuban government in 1979 to permit the visits by exiles.

These people who favor change have been joined generally in their demands by several liberal interest groups whose members have ties to leading universities, churches, research institutes, and human rights organizations. Notably, the largest and oldest Hispanic organization in the United States, the League of United Latin American Citizens (LULAC), supports the normalization of relations between Cuba and the United States.

Since 1980, however, some of the energies of these groups have been directed more toward U.S. policy in Central America than to Cuba. Other groups have altered their proposals, searching for minimal policy changes that might be acceptable in the face of the Reagan administration propaganda war against Cuba. For example, in 1984 the Inter-American Dialogue, cochaired by former Ambassador Sol M. Linowitz and former OAS Secretary General Galo Plaza, recommended little more than a "dialogue . . . between the United States and Cuba," especially over hostilities in Central America. Nine years earlier, a similar group headed by Linowitz called on the United States to "take the initiative in seeking a more normal relationship with Cuba . . . [and] to end the trade embargo."[8]

In early 1985, five U.S. Catholic leaders visited Cuba and met with Fidel Castro. The group included Bishop James Malone, president of the National Conference of Catholic Bishops, and Archbishop Patrick Flores, chairman of the bishops' committee on Latin America. It was the first high-level Catholic delegation from the United States since 1959.[9] Though no agreements were reached, the cordial meetings signalled a willingness on the bishops' part to consider including—as an element in their approach to peace in Central America—a call for dialogue between the United States and Cuba. The bishops have had influence in constraining the militarism of U.S. policy in Central America, and their voice in the Cuba debate, albeit tentative now, could have an impact.

Some companies have sought to lift the embargo in order to benefit from the renewed commerce. But recently their ardor has been diminished by several factors. Most have a concern about appearing unpatriotic, and official hostility toward Cuba has made business executives shy. The Reagan administration's posture has also made the exploration for markets in Cuba seem like a futile effort. Finally, conditions in Cuba appear to reduce the size of the likely market for U.S. business. Depressed world market prices have weakened Cuba's ability to earn hard currency for its products, and it already has some difficulty in repaying its more than \$3 billion foreign debt.[10] Still, at least 15 percent of Cuban imports originate in the West, and the third party congress called for this to grow to 20 percent. Such a posture gives U.S. business the continuing prospect of a market there.

The Balance of Forces

The ultimate strength of groups that oppose a change in policy is simultaneously the weakness of those that advocate change. The anticommunist crusade in Washington lends credibility and force to the campaign against communist Cuba and provides it with natural allies among conservative organizations that vigorously propound a militant cold war posture.[11] Normalization of relations with Cuba would not *inevitably* spark a wildfire against a president who initiated such a change, because anti-Cuban groups alone do not have the force to ignite it. But if conservative groups focused on a Cuba initiative as a symbol, they could create a major political obstacle. In 1977, the Panama Canal Treaty became such a symbol, and the new Carter administration had to expend significant political capital to gain Senate approval for ratification. In part, Carter's problem was that he created too few initiatives at the time, and this enabled conservative forces to focus their energy on the canal treaty. The key, then, to a successful Cuban initiative is for it to be one of many.

There is also a reciprocal relationship between groups and policy-makers. As officials need strong groups that bolster their efforts for change, so too do advocates need willing policymakers to whom they can appeal. Thus the atmosphere created by the executive and Congress can significantly determine the effectiveness of interest group pressure.

U.S. Congress

From a distance, recent congressional action on Cuba might appear as aggressive as that of the administration. In reality, the Congress has tended to modify the executive's bellicosity. Although it is likely that Congress will continue to do so, it is unlikely that the legislature itself would attempt to initiate a change in U.S. policy toward Cuba.

Consider the 1982 Symms amendment, which reaffirmed the 1962 threat to use force against Cuba. The Senate Foreign Relations Committee rejected it early in 1982, after a session during which even Republicans ridiculed its purpose.[12] Senator Steven Symms (R-

Idaho) reintroduced the legislation late in the session, on the floor, close to the midterm election. Under those circumstances it passed the Senate, and the House quietly concurred in conference. But the same day, the Senate also passed a resolution, by a vote of 97 to 2, to clarify that the Symms amendment "does not constitute the statutory authorization for the introduction of United States Armed Forces contemplated by the war powers resolution."[13]

Similarly, the Radio Marti that emerged from two years of legislative battle was intended to be less belligerent than the version President Reagan originally proposed. Instead of a separate station under the Board for International Broadcasting, Congress approved fourteen hours of Voice of America (VOA) broadcasts earmarked for Cuba. To be sure, the Cuban government perceived the special programs even under VOA auspices to be a very hostile act. The Radio Marti case thus suggests that congressional efforts at moderation may not be strong enough. Yet it also indicates that there would exist in Congress a base of support for a presidential initiative to reduce tensions with Cuba.

This base would include representatives and senators who have been outspoken in favor of a new dialogue with Cuba, such as representatives William Alexander (D-Ark.) and James Leach (R-Iowa), the latter a member of the Foreign Affairs Committee. Following a trip to Cuba in January 1985, they called for the president to open discussions with Cuba on a range of issues, including major ones that stand in the way of normal relations.[14] A few members of the congressional Black Caucus, especially Ronald Dellums (D-Calif.) and Mickey Leland (D-Texas), have traveled to Cuba in recent years, and many have advocated the normalization of relations. In the Senate, Claiborne Pell (D-R.I.), chair of the Senate Foreign Relations Committee, consistently has attempted to moderate presidential bellicosity toward Cuba. In fact, he placed improved relations with Cuba high on the agenda of goals he hopes to achieve.[15] On the Republican side, Lowell Weicker (R-Conn.) has actively supported negotiations between the two countries and has also traveled to Cuba.

The most formidable congressional adversary of normal relations with Cuba is Dante Fascell (D-Fla.), chair of the House Foreign Affairs Committee. He represents a district heavily populated with Cuban exiles and in the past has successfully stifled legislative steps to improve relations. But Fascell also has said that he believes the president should determine foreign policy, and this might mean that he would give a president some leeway in shaping policy toward Cuba. Senator Jesse Helms (R-N.C.) was an outspoken advocate of military action against Cuba when he was chair of the Senate Western Hemispheric Affairs Subcommittee.[16] But the change in party control of the Senate to the Democrats has significantly diminished his influence and opened the way for moderate senators—such as Christopher Dodd (D-Conn.), the current chair of the Western Hemispheric Affairs Subcommittee—to gain greater voice on the issue.

The lineup in Congress thus suggests it will continue to be a moderating force, though little more, on the Cuba policy. Whereas members have firmly avowed their opposition to military force against Cuba, most have not attacked the administration's efforts to tighten the embargo or to isolate Cuba diplomatically. Ultimately, Congress's role may depend on external events and on the administration's reaction to them. In the 1973 to 1975 period, Congress took a lead on normalizing relations because the president was unresponsive to entreaties from Latin American countries about U.S. Cuba policy. It could play that role again, especially if there were a public perception that the president's inflexibility could damage U.S. interests and involve the United States in conflict.

Press and Public Opinion

Presidents and members of Congress often blame the press and public opinion for pressuring them to take hard-line positions against communist countries. The press, they claim, searches for sensational stories and can rely on the wellspring of anticommunism, which has been nurtured in the public for much of the century, to inflame opinion against conciliatory gestures. This fear of an allegedly fickle public was captured succinctly in a remark by House Speaker Thomas P. O'Neill (D-Mass.), after Nicaraguan President Daniel Ortega traveled to Moscow following the congressional vote against aid. O'Neill said that he expected the House to vote in favor of aid to the anti-Nicaraguan guerrillas in the future—despite public opinion against such aid and the lack of consistency such a vote would entail—because Ortega "embarrassed us," and members felt that they then had to protect themselves.

A similar outlook prevails with respect to Cuba policy, a fear of the press and public. However, in both instances the fears are not well founded. Public opinion has been remarkably stable over the question of whether the United States should enter into negotiations with Cuba. In a 1977 nationwide poll, at the height of the Carter rapprochement, 59 percent favored "entering into negotiations with Cuba looking toward re-establishing . . . relations." Twenty-five percent were opposed. In a late 1982 poll, 48 percent favored negotiations to reestablish relations, as against 37 percent who were opposed. Among "opinion leaders," the margin was even greater in favor, 81 percent to 18 percent.[17]

Since the détente with Cuba in the mid-1970s, the press also has not followed its stereotypical pattern. This is especially noticeable in the face of the current U.S. propaganda effort because the press has reported fairly on Cuban overtures for negotiations, has questioned allegations that Cuban arms flow to guerrillas in El Salvador, and has featured Cuban speeches and claims that attacked the official U.S. version of the Grenada invasion.

The press and public opinion would thus appear to provide opportunities for leaders who might want to change U.S. policy toward Cuba. Though they could hardly be counted as forces for change, they are not entrenched against such change.

A Relatively Open Field

This overview of the domestic political landscape indicates that it neither provides overwhelming obstacles to thwart a new Cuba policy, nor does it have many downhill slides to make the development of such a policy easy. What it offers is a relatively free area in which a president can move.

The most ardent anti-Cuban interest groups are located in only two states, Florida and New Jersey, though with their campaign funds collected through their political action committees they may gain some footing elsewhere. Less ideological groups might be satisfied with gains that could come from negotiations. Some members of Congress might be able to thwart full normal relations. But much could be accomplished in reducing tension without even relying on the Congress. A president has the authority to relax or even end the embargo without congressional approval and could negotiate executive agreements on several bilateral issues. Moreover, such efforts would have some support in the legislature, as well as in the public at large. Thus the call for a new policy toward Cuba need not be seen as a visionary proposal, and it is consistent with the domestic political reality of the United States.

Notes

1. Helga Silva and Guy Gugliotta, "'La Causa' Binds Exile Community," *Miami Herald,* December 11, 1983, pp. 14M–15M; Lourdes Arguelles, "Miami's

Cubans: Illicit Heritage, Uncertain Future," *CubaTimes,* Spring 1982, pp. 27–31.

2. R. A. Zaldivar, "Miami Cubans Build Powerful Lobby Group," *Miami Herald,* August 11, 1986, p. 1; Guillermo Martinez, "Cuban Exiles Pour Money into Congressional Races," *Miami Herald,* September 27, 1982.

3. Jon Nordheimer, "Cuban-American Leader Builds a Foundation of Power Beyond Miami," *New York Times,* July 12, 1986, p. 6. However, the CANF has strongly backed Rep. Dante Fascell (D-Fla.), and its advisory council has members affiliated with the Democratic party.

4. In a 1983 poll of Miami Cubans, a majority opposed the resumption of diplomatic relations by a 68–23 margin. But they divided more evenly on the question of whether Cuban-Americans should travel to Cuba, with 50 percent saying they should not and 42 percent saying they should travel. See "Fall Survey—Questions, Responses," *Miami Herald,* December 18, 1983, p. 8M.

5. Alfred L. Padula, Jr., "U.S. Business Squabbles Over Cuba," *Nation,* October 22, 1977, pp. 391–392.

6. Their views can be found in the magazine *Areito.*

7. Maria Torres, "From Exiles to Minorities: The Politics of the Cuban Political Community in the United States," Ph.D. Dissertation, University of Michigan, 1986.

8. Inter-American Dialogue, *The Americas in 1984: A Year for Decisions* (Washington, D.C.: Aspen Institute for Humanistic Studies, 1984), p. 35; Commission on U.S.–Latin American Relations, *The Americas in a Changing World* (New York: Quadrangle, 1975), p. 29.

9. Julia Preston, "U.S. Clerics Get Lecture from Castro," *Miami Herald,* January 25, 1985.

10. Karen DeYoung, "Cuba's Trade Troubles Bring Economic Change," *Washington Post,* February 4, 1985. Also see Lawrence Theriot, "Cuba Faces the Economic Realities of the 1980s," U.S. Congress, Joint Economic Committee, 97th Cong., 2nd Sess., March 22, 1982.

11. Philip Brenner, "Waging Ideological War: Anti-Communism and U.S. Policy in Central America," *The Socialist Register 1984* (London: Merlin Press, 1984), pp. 246–251.

12. *Congressional Quarterly Weekly Report,* May 1, 1982, pp. 1009–1010.

13. The resolution was offered by Sen. Dale Bumpers (D-Ark.); *Congressional Record,* August 11, 1982, pp. S10226–S10233.

14. R. A. Zaldivar, "2 Congressmen Find Castro 'Conciliatory,' Set to Talk," *Miami Herald,* January 18, 1985, p. 17A. Also see Joanne Omang, "Democratic Party Urged to Convene Hemispheric Meeting, Invite Cuba," *Washington Post,* January 24, 1985, p. A26; William V. Alexander, Jr., "Let's Talk With Castro," *New York Times,* February 14, 1985.

15. Bernard Weinraub, "New Foreign Relations Chief Is Not a Cream Puff," *New York Times,* February 3, 1987, p. A18.

16. Alfonso Chardy, "Conservative Pressure Brings U.S. Review of '62 Accords on Cuba," *Miami Herald,* July 7, 1983, p. 12A.

17. William Watts and Jorge I. Dominguez, *The United States and Cuba: Old Issues and New Directions,* (Washington, D.C.: Potomac Associates, 1977), p. 60; John E. Reilly, *American Public Opinion and U.S. Foreign Policy 1983* (Chicago: Chicago Council on Foreign Relations, 1983), p. 20.

CHAPTER 6

A Sensible Policy

GEORGE WASHINGTON PRESCRIBED a guideline for U.S. foreign policy that, until recently, had been our national good sense. He advised that we avoid permanent entangling alliances, and conversely, permanent antagonisms. With Cuba we have ignored his admonitions. As a result, after thirty years of hostility directed at its neighbor, the United States appears more like a vindictive petty power than a mature superpower. It is time to restore common sense to our Cuba policy.

A Failed Policy

Unattained Objectives

The Cuba policy of the United States has failed to achieve any of its objectives. Cuba's government has withstood the direct U.S. attacks on it: invasion, sabotage, and assassination attempts. The economic embargo has made the average Cuban's life more difficult, but it has neither destroyed the economy nor stopped the Cubans from developing their country. Efforts to isolate and contain Cuba have succeeded in reducing Cuban contact with the West for short periods. But their ultimate purpose of destabilizing the government obviously has failed.

Meanwhile, the current manifestation of this three-decade policy has even undermined the Reagan administration's particular objectives. The administration has said it wants Cuba to cut its ties to the Soviet Union, to end its support for both the Nicaraguan government and the guerrillas in El Salvador, and to remove its troops from Angola. In each case, U.S. policy operates against these immediate goals.

81

Relations with the Soviet Union. The "special relationship with the Soviet Union," the head of the State Department's Cuba Desk asserted in 1984, is "the first and most critical" concern for the United States in considering relations with Cuba. It is a relationship, he added, on which the Reagan administration does not believe the United States can have much influence.[1] This is certain to be the case if the United States maintains a hostile posture toward Cuba. In the face of such U.S. animosity, Cuba not only has no incentive to reduce its tie to the Soviet Union and Eastern bloc, but also would be undermining its national security if it cut off the source of economic and military assistance.

Central America. Administration officials regularly link their concern about instability in Central America to Soviet and Cuban activities in the area. In part, they argue, Soviet military assistance provided through Cuba adds a global strategic dimension to the local conflicts, because Soviet bases in Central America could threaten the ability of the United States to respond appropriately to its international interests. Cuba itself, officials charge, has exacerbated regional tension through its support for insurgencies.[2] Yet the Reagan administration's militaristic approach to the conflicts in the region and its focus on the Cuban presence as an excuse for U.S. intervention have little chance of bringing stability to the region or of reducing the Cuban presence in Central America.

Cuba, too, has an interest in ending the conflicts in Central America. It fears that prolonged war there could lead to massive U.S. military intervention. At the least, that would polarize Latin America and affect Cuba's efforts to reestablish normal relations with countries in the hemisphere. Even worse, U.S. intervention could draw Cuba into a direct confrontation with the United States, as Cuba has military advisers, teachers, and technicians in Nicaragua.

The major Latin American countries with which Cuba seeks better relations all want negotiated settlements in Central America that will take into account U.S. security concerns. This has encouraged Cuba's recent tendency to moderation. It should be stressed that Cuba repeatedly endorsed the Contadora principles for a Central American peace treaty proposed by Mexico, Panama, Colombia, and Venezuela and said it would abide by plans that require the removal of all foreign militaries from Central America. Similarly, it has supported the peace treaty proposed by Costa Rican President Oscar Arias and signed by the Central American countries in August 1987.

Angola. Current U.S. policy offers Cuba little reason to reduce its force in or to leave Angola. Cuba's military support for Angola has not been costly because the Angolans have paid Cuba for the cost of maintaining the troops and the Soviets provide for their transportation.[3] Moreover, as South Africa further alienates itself from the world community, Cuba gains from its staunch resistance to South African pressure against Angola. By focusing the issue on Cuban troops in the region, the United States appears tacitly to endorse South Africa's violation of UN Security Council Resolution 435 and incursions into Angola. Indeed, U.S. aid to the UNITA guerrillas in Angola, who receive significant support from South Africa, allies the United States with South Africa in the war against Angola. The impetus for U.S. aid comes in part from pressure by anti-Castro members of Congress who see such support as an indirect way of attacking Cuba.[4] The dogmatic anti-Cuban U.S. approach thus undermines efforts to resolve the region's conflicts and places the United States on the side of one of the world's most reviled regimes.

Costs of Failure

To perpetuate such a failed policy has significant costs for the United States, beyond the loss of immediate objectives. The policy threatens U.S. interests with respect to its allies. It infects domestic U.S. politics with a cold war emotionalism, which has the dangerous potential to increase tension in the Third World: When the United States defines regional or North-South problems as aspects of an East-West conflict, it makes a wider war all the more likely. Ultimately, the policy undermines the rule of law, which is the only sane framework to guide the international relations of the United States.

Allies. Nearly every important U.S. ally maintains normal diplomatic and trade relations with Cuba. This has generated some tension in the alliance, particularly when the United States has attempted to tighten the embargo and restrict trade between Cuba and U.S. allies. Such interference is felt most keenly by Latin American countries. In fact, in a March 1987 vote, several of them refused to support a U.S. resolution against Cuba in the UN Human Rights Commission, despite intensive lobbying by the United States.[5]

The allies reject the dogmatic anticommunism with which the United States has shaped its Cuba policy. They have been better able to satisfy their own interests vis-à-vis Cuba with negotiations and diplomacy than with confrontation. They do not perceive Cuba as a threat to vital U.S. interests, and they consider the United States to have undermined its own interests in pursuit of an ideologically based policy. This difference in perception costs the United States credibility because the United States is seen as irrational about Cuba.[6]

Cold War Politics. A rational calculation of U.S. interests vis-à-vis Cuba has been difficult because of the emotion-laden rhetoric used to discuss Cuba. This political rhetoric contributes to a cold war atmosphere within the United States that makes elected officials fearful that unscrupulous opponents will tar them with the label "soft on communism." Similar red-baiting discourages policymakers in the State or Defense departments from proposing nonbelligerent approaches to Cuba. Indeed, in order to demonstrate their resolve against communism, elected and nonelected officials have supported illegal and questionable actions against countries with close ties to Cuba, such as Nicaragua and Grenada.

Cold war politics engenders a mentality of "us versus them," which discourages domestic political dissent. The antagonist is depicted as a demonic evil, which makes negotiation futile. Treaties that allow the enemy to survive are not satisfactory. Total victory over evil becomes the only acceptable alternative, and this encourages talk of military solutions, which further narrows political debate.

Third World Politics. Military approaches to Third World political problems offer the most dangerous and least successful solutions. The problems rarely arise from clear territorial dispute, which military might can sometimes settle, but more often involve basic conflicts over a way of life. By describing such struggles in East-West terms, which often occurs when the Cubans are involved, the United States needlessly raises the stakes to the level of vital interest.

The Soviet Union also has interests in the Third World, many of which can be accommodated with U.S. interests. But when the United States poses its interest as vital, it offers less room for mutual accommodation. In turn, regional clashes become potential flash points for a direct confrontation between the two superpowers. This is precisely the kind of escalation that the United States needs to avoid to maintain a stable and peaceful world.

Most U.S. leaders appreciate this danger, which is one reason they have resorted to covert and surrogate military involvement in the Third World. Through covert action and the reliance on surrogates, such as the Contras, the United States maintains the fiction that it is not really involved in a conflict. But it is a fiction that fools no one. It merely makes the U.S. Congress and U.S. allies party to illegal actions, and undermines the legitimacy of both domestic and international institutions.

Rule of Law. The Iran-Contra scandal of 1987 highlights the folly of such evasions of the law. U.S. involvement in Third World conflicts, in the pursuit of imaginary East-West gains, has little domestic support. To pursue such involvement, U.S. officials find they need to bend and finally break the law. They sometimes rely on other lawbreakers—drug dealers, terrorists, merchants of illegal arms—who know how to operate in the underworld. This makes the United States an accomplice to their nefarious acts and undermines the rule of law at home.

Similarly, the efforts to circumvent basic international charters to which the United States is a signatory and that require the United States to respect the sovereignty of other countries undermine the international order. Because the United States is a world power, its behavior sets a tone for the world community. To the extent that the U.S. relationship with Cuba is a model of great power–small power interaction, the United States is encouraging a resort to force in international affairs. This is a cost the United States must avoid. Given its interests around the globe, it should seek to have diplomacy replace armed conflict. Otherwise the United States is likely to be drawn into needless wars wherever it has interests at stake.

A New Policy

New Objectives

Current U.S. policy toward Cuba has failed because its objectives are inconsistent with basic U.S. values and interests. The United States has stood for honesty and the rule of law, for pluralism and tolerance, and for peace and the diplomatic resolution of conflicts. U.S. foreign policy is strongest when it extends, not when it overturns, traditions that the U.S. public holds dear; the policy is most likely to be successful when it is rooted in reality, not lies and distortions.

To replace the outworn framework of its Cuba policy, the United States should adopt four new objectives that are consistent with basic U.S. values and interests: the enhancement of national security, the promotion of peace and stability, the attainment of development with equity, and the realization of democracy and human rights.[7]

Security. The United States has an interest in diminishing the possibility of confrontation with the Soviet Union in the region. A collateral interest is to reduce the Soviet *military* presence in the hemisphere in order to decrease the number of flash points that could lead to conflict.

U.S. security is not undermined automatically when a nearby country has economic and political relations with the Soviet Union. Several countries in Latin America already trade extensively with the Soviet Union and its allies. Virtually no country in the hemisphere supports the United States more than 25 percent of the time in the United Nations.

Cuba's military reliance on the Soviet Union is very much a function of the Cuban perception that the United States threatens the island. In this decade, Cuba requested significantly expanded military assistance from the Soviet Union in the face of increased hostility from the United States. In fact, Cuba refuses to sign any agreement under which it would be forced to renounce the right to have nuclear weapons because of national security considerations.[8]

A serious U.S. promise to respect Cuba's right to exist could lead to a reduction in the Soviet military presence there. Indeed, Cuba recognizes that if there were a conflict between the United States and the Soviet Union, the military installations in Cuba—if not the country itself—would be the first target for destruction by U.S. forces. For this reason, it has an interest in diminishing its military ties to the Soviet Union.

During the past thirty years, the United States has come to accept some pluralism in the region because the United States now realizes it cannot control the behavior of every country. The very effort to exert total control undermines U.S. security because it alienates sovereign allies, it disrupts the inter-American system, and it extends the United States beyond its means and capability. The time has come, finally, to apply this realism to Cuba.

Stability. Although the United States has acted as if it is the only country with hemispheric interests, all countries in the region perceive that they too have a stake in it. This was the impetus for the initial Contadora meeting between Mexico, Panama, Colombia, and Venezuela. Latin Americans themselves sought a way to end the bloodshed in Central America and to ward off possible U.S. military intervention. This perception continues to motivate their efforts to resolve the conflicts there. Peace and stability can be achieved in the region only by including every country that is both involved and feels its interests are at stake. There are regional and North-South issues that do not fit into an East-West framework. As more countries reestablish normal relations with Cuba in pursuit of their own regional interests, the exclusion of Cuba from hemispheric consultation impedes any effort to generate a stable peace.

Stability would also be enhanced if countries in the region could rely on the United States to be a consistent adherent to the law. Direct U.S. support for the overthrow of regimes in the hemisphere feeds the ambitions of authoritarian plotters, who hope the United States will support their attacks on legitimate governments. Their hope often has rested on their credentials as virulent anticommunists.

But normal relations between the United States and Cuba could send a signal through the region that the United States has abandoned its fanatical anticommunism, and it could serve to discourage those who would undermine stability.

Development. As even the 1984 Kissinger Commission recognized, poverty and inequality are the root causes of turmoil in Latin America. The Cuban model of development is not wholly relevant for each country or even adaptable to some. But Cuba has had some remarkable successes: Its population is the healthiest of any Latin American country, it has ended malnutrition and hunger, and its literacy rate is over 90 percent.[9] To the extent that the United States tries to make Cuba a pariah, it denies the legitimacy of the Cuban model and robs countries of the chance to exchange information that could be beneficial to all of them.

The Caribbean Basin is Cuba's natural trading area. Cubans have skills and resources with which they can make a positive contribution to regional development. This could be accomplished if the United States encouraged Cuban economic reintegration into the region. A salutary benefit might be that Cuba could, in this way, diversify its dependency and reduce its trade with the Soviet bloc. Indeed, its current economic plan calls for growth in trade with Western countries.

Democracy and Human Rights. The United States should respect each country's sovereignty and rely on international organizations such as the Human Rights Commission of the OAS to secure its humanitarian concerns. To the extent that these agencies are not effective, the United States should work to strengthen them. One route to improving such organs would be to involve all countries in their work, including Cuba.

Cuba's suppression of important political rights has been largely a function of its quest for security, which is fueled by U.S. threats. During the Carter administration, when there was the beginning of a rapprochement, some internal controls were significantly relaxed. A large number of political prisoners were released during this period, and Cuba permitted the start of a massive program for humanitarian visits by exile families.[10] This program did lead to some internal disruption, and it was significantly cut back as tension heightened under the Reagan administration.

People-to-people exchanges, which become possible in a meaningful way only if there is movement toward normalization, can significantly reduce tension and could help to open the Cuban system. This is already evident from visits to Cuba by U.S. church representatives. They have helped to enhance the legitimacy of the

Cuban churches, which in turn has contributed to an increased pluralism.

A New Attitude

Recognize Cuba's Sovereignty. The first step toward establishing a new Cuba policy would be to accept the reality that Cuba is a sovereign country. It has the right to organize itself as a communist state, uncontrolled by the United States, and to relate freely to other sovereign states. The signal of this new attitude would come when the United States lowered the wall of hostility it has erected around Cuba, because the animosity has been intended to isolate and destabilize Cuba.

At the same time, the United States should end the propaganda war aimed at blackening Cuba's image in the eyes of the U.S. people. This new attitude would likely be well received in Cuba, and U.S. officials could reasonably expect that Cuba would signal its receptivity by modifying its rhetoric against the United States. Cuban leaders have said that an end to U.S. animosity is the only precondition they place on negotiations with the United States.

Not only is the time long past when the United States could hope to restore Cuba to a pre-1959, semicolonial bastion responsive to U.S. dictates. The United States should abandon such hopes in general and frame its foreign policy in accord with international law and internationally recognized rules of conduct.

Cuba is a stable country with which most of the countries in the world have normal relations. As a close neighbor, ninety miles away, the United States has a special obligation to work out a way of living with Cuba. To accept the premise that Cuba has a right to exist would not require the United States to relinquish its interest in security or its responsibility to fulfill obligations under mutual defense pacts. It would mean that the United States could not threaten Cuba's own security.

Remove Restrictions on the Free Exchange of Ideas. An important signal of a new U.S. attitude would be the expansion of communication between the people of the United States and Cuba. The Reagan administration has severely restricted this sort of communication. It curtailed travel to Cuba by most people in the United States in 1982 when the Treasury Department reinstituted a prohibition on the expenditure of money in Cuba by U.S. citizens.[11] It tried to ban the importation of Cuban publications into the United States, and despite its failure to impose this restriction, the attempt may have intimidated people from seeking Cuban publications. In a 1985 presidential proclamation, Reagan announced the general denial of visas to any Cuban who had ever traveled abroad on an official government passport or who was a member of the Communist party. In effect, this denied entry to the United States to virtually all Cuban scholars, scientists, journalists, and artists. The U.S. public's opportunity to question, challenge, and exchange information with Cubans has been lost. Moreover, the proclamation killed several promising university exchange programs because they were based on reciprocal invitations.

The removal of these restrictions would enable U.S. citizens to be better informed. Cubans would be able to attend U.S. universities, to participate in professional conferences, and to speak at public forums. It would allow cultural exchanges to develop and expand, including the exchange of information between scholars. It would end a significant infringement on the First Amendment guarantee that a U.S. citizen has a right to travel. Delegations of professionals, church groups, students, and businesspeople from the United States could add to the impetus within Cuba for even greater receptivity toward contact with the United States.

Normalizing Relations

Two lessons stand out from prior efforts at accommodation. First, delay works against the process, because domestic political opposition builds as the process goes forward. Second, political leaders should not raise public expectations too high. The antagonisms and differences between the United States and Cuba have been built up over many years and run deep. Many of these are likely to remain, even after a normal relationship is established.

Despite the desirability of speed, all of the steps needed to achieve the objectives of a new policy need not be taken instantaneously. The process could begin with small steps, although several of these should be taken at the same time.

The normalization process itself is an ongoing relationship between two countries. It would be distinguished from the current relationship by virtue of the mutual intention to establish full commercial and diplomatic relations and by the mutual commitment to work out differences through peaceful means. The process would be stimulated as both countries took meaningful actions to address the interests that each has articulated. The following proposals indicate ways in which it might proceed.

Engage in Direct Negotiations with Cuba over Common Interests. Both countries could benefit by the settlement of minor bilateral differences through mutual accommodation. Even during periods of heightened animosity, there have been negotiations and agreements over bilateral issues. In 1973 the United States and Cuba signed an antihijacking agreement, and in 1984 they reached an accord on immigration. As recently as 1986 there were preliminary talks over the highly charged question of Radio Marti broadcasts.

Officials in both countries have suggested that the issues that would be candidates for such talks would include: fishing rights in boundary waters; common efforts to control the international movement of narcotics; common efforts to combat international terrorism; the relaxation of limitations each country places on diplomatic personnel serving in the respective interests sections; the size of each diplomatic mission; and radio and television transmissions, such as Radio Marti, which each country might broadcast to the other.

Through the linking of several concerns, trade-offs may be facilitated and the interests of domestic groups more easily accommodated. Success on these matters would lower the level of distrust between the countries, as well as the atmosphere of confrontation. Success also could enable the United States to move on to issues around which mutual accommodation would be more difficult.

Open Two-Way Trade Between the United States and Cuba. An end to the economic embargo against Cuba would be an important way to reduce tension between the countries. A partial lifting of the trade restrictions could occur first on a humanitarian basis, enabling Cuba to purchase food and medicine from the United States. This is likely to generate only minimal trade because Cuba already can purchase most of the medicine it needs from other countries. Yet Cuba might shift the source of some of its food imports such as rice to U.S. exporters, which would benefit farmers in Arkansas and Louisiana.

To make the action reciprocal, the trade could not be only one-way; Cuban products would need to be permitted access to the U.S. market. Candidates for such commerce would be tobacco and seafood. Cuba would be unlikely to seek the sale of sugar, nickel, and citrus to the United States immediately because virtually all of its output in these products is earmarked to fulfill existing obligations. As relations improved over the years, there could be negotiations to grant Cuba both a portion of the U.S. sugar quota and the ability to sell citrus in a way that would not harm U.S. domestic growers.

Among the obstacles to a resumption of trade between the United States and Cuba are the outstanding claims for property damage each country has against the other. Yet Cuba has successfully settled such claims with other countries, and it is willing to discuss this issue. Indeed, compensation to former owners of property that Cuba nationalized is likely only if there is a movement toward normalization.

Estimates of the potential trade between the United States and Cuba depend on assumptions about the future of the Cuban economy and on Cuba's willingness to substitute U.S. goods for those it now receives from other Western countries. Approximately 15 percent of Cuba's foreign trade today is with the West, for which it needs hard currency. Although it has set 20 percent as the 1990 goal for trade with the West, Cuba may not be able to generate sufficient hard currency from the sale of its products abroad. This would limit what it could purchase from the United States. Moreover, as Cuba developed its infrastructure after 1961 with machinery made outside the United States, its need for U.S. spare parts correspondingly diminished. In part, then, the level of trade would reflect a political decision by Cuba to trade with the United States for goods it already buys from other sources.[12]

The United States still remains the best source for high technology. Cuba has placed a great emphasis recently on developing industries based on high technology and allegedly has gone to great lengths to obtain U.S. technology through third countries and state corporations disguised as private entities. Given the lower shipping costs for other products, too, there is likely to be a market of several hundred million dollars in Cuba. Regular commercial transactions would thus benefit both countries.

Involve Cuba in Multilateral Negotiations. Both Cuba and the United States have interests at stake in the hemisphere. Cuba's relations with countries in Latin America have been improving steadily during the 1980s. As the United States works with these countries to implement new development plans, Cuba should be included in the regional discussions and programs. It is a natural trading partner and has successfully implemented programs that might be tried elsewhere. The exclusion of Cuba needlessly encumbers developmental efforts because regional ties with Cuba cannot be taken into appropriate account.

Similarly, both countries have an interest in a viable solution to the Latin American debt crisis. As the countries in the hemisphere attempt to develop such a plan, the United States will inevitably be involved in multilateral forums on the debt because it is the largest creditor nation for Latin America. All hemispheric countries should be invited to participate in order to make the solution universally applicable and acceptable. The United States should welcome, not obstruct, Cuban participation.

Joint efforts of this sort could begin to bring Cuba back into the inter-American system. As a member of the inter-American community, Cuba might be willing then to participate in multilateral political processes, such as those of international organizations that attempt to improve human rights in the hemisphere. Such participation could even lead Cuba to sign the Treaty of Tlatelolco, which bars the introduction or development of nuclear weapons in the hemisphere.

As the United States and Cuba work together on problems, their negotiations could provide the basis for further dialogue. Reduced tension in the hemisphere would enable elected officials to appeal to the antiwar sentiment of their constituents and to diffuse the atavistic demands of extremists in the Cuban-American community. In this way discussions with Cuba over issues unrelated directly to normalization may help not only to reduce mutual distrust. They could also enhance support for further talks by vitiating some domestic political opposition to negotiations with Cuba.

Negotiate a Nonaggression Pact. Cuban fears of a U.S. invasion may be unrealistic. But they are rooted in the memory of the series of U.S. military occupations early in the century and in the 1961 U.S.-sponsored Bay of Pigs invasion. These fears are fueled by continuing U.S. military overflights of the island, hostile military exercises off the Cuban coast, and occasional threats by senior U.S. officials to attack Cuba.

These provocations only increase tension in the region and serve no U.S. interest. They are a barrier to negotiations; they force Cuba to rely on the Soviet Union to help in maintaining and modernizing a large military force; and they engender within Cuba a wartime posture that reinforces restrictions on freedoms. U.S. security was not impaired when such overt hostility was relaxed during the Carter administration.

The United States might unilaterally discontinue its provocative military activities. Alternatively, it might seek to negotiate a non-aggression pact with Cuba. Such a pact could include U.S. recognition of Cuba's right to exist. Although this action undoubtedly would anger extremist Cuban-American interest groups, security-oriented members of Congress might find such an agreement appealing. It would also be received well by the public at large because the agreement would reduce tension between the countries.

Negotiate the Reduction of Foreign Military Forces. Cuba has never ruled out the possibility of altering its military relationship with the Soviet Union. But it has had little reason to do so while it felt threatened by the United States. The end of hostile U.S. military actions and a nonaggression pact could begin to increase Cuba's sense of security and open the way for negotiations over the extent of the Soviet military presence in Cuba.

Cuba might countenance, for example, the removal of Soviet reconnaissance aircraft, such as the surveillance version of the Bear bomber. These provide little benefit to the Soviet Union while they generate some discomfort for the United States.[13] The Soviets might also be willing to reduce their troop presence on the island. The 3,000-soldier Soviet brigade was first placed in Cuba during the 1962 Cuban missile crisis to act as a type of trip wire against a possible U.S. invasion. Were the likelihood of an invasion reduced, the logic of maintaining the brigade would be reduced accordingly.

In turn, the United States could offer to remove its own forces from Cuba. These are stationed at Guantanamo Naval Base, which the United States built during its occupation of Cuba in the early twentieth century. The base is obviously vulnerable and thus provides little strategic benefit for the United States. But it does engender some insecurity on Cuba's part and stands out as a constant reminder of the prior U.S. imperial presence.

To be sure, Cuba would need to consult closely with the Soviet Union on such trade-offs. Yet the Soviet Union might be quite ready to acquiesce if it saw its own interests as unharmed and perceived that a reduction of its force would further diminish the possibility of a U.S.-Cuban military confrontation. Moreover, it is unlikely that Cuba would sever all military ties to the Soviet Union even if relations with the United States were cordial.

Begin Discussions over International Issues. U.S. officials have asserted that Cuba's international behavior stands in the way of normalized relations between the two countries. Yet the United States disapproves of the behavior of many countries with which it has normal relations. Even allies have acted in ways that allegedly have harmed U.S. interests. The normal pattern of response is to seek a compromise, through bilateral or multilateral negotiations, or to accept the disagreeable behavior. When the United States has attempted to bully another country into submission, the effort often has backfired and the result has been the undermining of international trust and goodwill.

In Africa, Cuba and the United States support opposite sides of struggles in Angola, Namibia, South Africa, and Ethiopia. Cuba and the United States differ over questions about development assistance to the Third World and over the responsibilities of the advanced industrial nations. Cuba has supported liberation movements in several countries, at times against regimes to which the United States is tied. Of special concern, Cuba has backed the Puerto Rican independence movement despite vigorous U.S. protestations that the status of Puerto Rico is an internal affair of the United States.

None of these differences is susceptible to an easy reconciliation, and many would continue past the time when the two countries considered their relations to be normal. As part of the process of making those relations normal, the differences need to be adjudicated in ways that most countries of the world work on such conflicts— through negotiations.

Exchange Ambassadors and Open Regular Consular Offices. At the point when the two countries finally accord each other full diplomatic recognition, establish embassies, and open consular offices, the exchange of ambassadors would be almost symbolic. The process would have developed an ongoing, normal relationship between the United States and Cuba, based on mutual respect for each country's sovereignty and a mutual acknowledgment of each country's interests.

The Ball Is in Our Court

The United States has little to gain by maintaining its bellicose refusal to talk with Cuba. U.S. interests can be secured only by negotiating with Cuba. The November 1987 restoration of the immigration agreement is a case in point. The United States bargained skillfully and with little flexibility, but it did talk to Cuba. The result was the achievement of a U.S. objective. Some opponents of change say that negotiations would legitimate the Cuban government. But in the eyes of the world it is already legitimate. Others argue that the movement toward normalization would signify U.S. approval of practices by the Cuban government that we should not condone. Yet the United States has relations with virtually every other country in the world, many of whose actions we condemn.

Privately, some U.S. officials and members of Congress acknowledge that U.S. policy toward Cuba undermines U.S. interests and should be changed. They add, though, that political expedience dictates that they cannot advocate such a change. They fear that attacks by the Cuban-American community and by conservative organizations would force them from office or debilitate them politically. Although such attacks are likely to occur, the fears are exaggerated. The Cuban-American community is not monolithic, and several past campaigns by conservatives have failed to ignite a fire storm. Indeed, as the United States once again recognizes its best interest lies in talking to the Soviet Union, those who oppose negotiations with communists are the ones who seem to threaten U.S. security.

At one time the Cuban government resisted negotiations with the United States. It laid down preconditions to any talks, such as a demand for an end to the economic embargo. Today, changes within Cuba give it the strength to be flexible. Cuban leaders state that there are no preconditions anymore and that they are willing to discuss the broad range of issues that touch on all of the U.S. interests outlined here. They emphasize that the only obstacle to talks between the two countries is U.S. hostility. The ball is in the U.S. court.

The issues between the United States and Cuba are amenable to resolution if the United States approaches them realistically. The United States needs to relinquish the unrealistic goals of fundamentally changing Cuba and uncoupling it from the Soviet Union. Cuba will not bargain away its sovereignty, nor does the United States need to seek such a bargain. With attainable goals, there could be serious negotiations and tangible benefits for the United States. Indeed, only by talking to Cuba can the United States hope to achieve its interests.

Tension between the United States and Cuba is at one of its highest levels since 1959. Current U.S. policy only exacerbates this undesirable state of affairs. Now is the time to change the policy so that the two countries can relate to each other in ways that best serve their citizens. It is time to move from confrontation to negotiation.

Notes

1. Kenneth Skoug, "The United States and Cuba," Current Policy No. 646, December 17, 1984, U.S. Department of State, Bureau of Public Affairs, pp. 2, 3.

2. Ibid., p. 3; *Report of the National Bipartisan Commission on Central America* [Kissinger Commission], Washington, D.C., 1984, pp. 88–93; U.S. Departments of State and Defense, "The Soviet-Cuban Connection in Central America and the Caribbean," March 1985, pp. 3–10, 41.

3. According to Pamela Falk, the benefit to Cuba may have decreased recently because Angola's ability to pay Cuba in hard currency has diminished with the fall in the price of oil. See Pamela S. Falk, "Cuba in Africa," *Foreign Affairs,* vol. 65, no. 5, Summer 1987, p. 1095. However, this merely means that Cuba may receive less hard currency from Angola. Angola continues to bear the cost of maintaining Cuban troops there.

4. Steve Blakely, "House Hands Reagan Victory On 'Covert' Aid to Angolans," *Congressional Quarterly Weekly Report,* September 20, 1986, pp. 2202–2203.

5. Peter Slevin, "U.S. Tactics Backfired in Cuba Vote," *Miami Herald,* March 15, 1987, p. 1.

6. There is a parallel view of U.S. policy toward Nicaragua. See Daniel Siegel and Tom Spaulding, with Peter Kornbluh, "Outcast Among Allies," Institute for Policy Studies Issue Paper, Washington, D.C.: November 1985.

7. For a fuller discussion of these interests, see Policy Alternatives for the Caribbean and Central America (PACCA), *Changing Course: Blueprint for Peace in Central America and the Caribbean* (Washington, D.C.: Institute for Policy Studies, 1984), pp. 41–51.

8. Vice President Carlos Rafael Rodriguez declared on February 16, 1987, in an interview with a PACCA delegation consisting of Philip Brenner, Robert Stark, and Carmen Diana Deere, that Cuba has been unwilling to sign the treaty because it will not forgo the option of obtaining nuclear weapons to protect itself from a hostile United States. However, he did not specifically rule out the possibility that Cuba might be willing to sign this nonnuclear pact if the United States ended its hostility and sought normal relations.

9. Claus Brundenius, "Development Strategies and Basic Human Needs," in *The Cuba Reader,* ed. Philip Brenner, William M. LeoGrande, Donna Rich, and Daniel Siegel (New York: Grove, forthcoming); Medea Benjamin et al., *No Free Lunch* (San Francisco: Institute for Food and Development Policy, 1984), chapter 7.

10. Wayne S. Smith, *The Closest of Enemies* (New York: Norton, 1987), pp. 144–163.

11. There are four categories of U.S. nationals exempt from the ban: U.S. government officials, scholars, journalists, and Cuban exiles visiting their families.

12. Cuba made such a political decision in 1985 in the case of Brazil in order to forge closer ties, and it shifted millions of dollars in commerce from other trading partners to Brazil. See Mimi Whitefield, "After Thaw, Brazil-Cuba Trade Is Blooming," *Miami Herald,* November 10, 1986, Business Monday, p. 17.

13. For an interesting discussion of this idea, see Wayne S. Smith, "The Cuba-Soviet Alliance," paper prepared for Johns Hopkins University-DISEU Conference, March 19–23, 1986, Havana, Cuba, p. 12.

Chronology

1895

Apr. 15: Cuba's second war of independence began.

May 19: José Martí, poet and father of the Cuban independence movement, was killed in combat against the Spanish.

1898

Feb. 15: The U.S. battleship *Maine* exploded in Havana harbor.

Apr. 25: The United States declared war on Spain. (The Spanish-American war lasted three months and ended with a U.S. military occupation of Cuba.)

1901

May 28: At U.S. insistence, the Platt Amendment was added to the Cuban constitution. It limited Cuban sovereignty in dealings with other countries and gave the United States the right to intervene in Cuba at will.

1933

Aug. 12: The dictatorship of Gerardo Machado was overthrown by the "Revolution of '33."

1934

Jan. 16: At the instigation of U.S. Ambassador Sumner Welles, Ramón Grau San Martín, president of the revolutionary government, was forced out of office by the military, headed by Fulgencio Batista.

May 29: The Platt Amendment was abrogated.

A similar version of this chronology will appear in *The Cuba Reader,* ed. Philip Brenner, William LeoGrande, Donna Rich, and Daniel Siegel (New York: Grove Press, forthcoming). Used by permission.

1952

Mar. 10: Batista overthrew the government of Carlos Prío Socorrás.

1953

July 26: Led by Fidel Castro, 134 rebels attacked Moncada barracks in Santiago, marking the start of the insurrection against Batista. Most were killed or captured. (At his trial in September, Castro gave his famous speech, "History Will Absolve Me.")

1959

Jan. 1–2: Batista fled and rebel army troops under Ernesto "Che" Guevara entered Havana, marking the triumph of the revolution.

Feb. 16: Fidel Castro, commander of the rebel army, replaced Miró Cardona as prime minister of the revolutionary government.

Apr. 15–26: Castro traveled to the United States at the invitation of the Association of Newspaper Editors and met with Vice President Richard Nixon (who later in the year urged that the United States begin planning a paramilitary covert operation to oust Castro).

May 17: The first Agrarian Reform Law was promulgated, nationalizing about one-third of the arable land in Cuba. (Compensation for the property of U.S. citizens affected by the law became a major point of controversy in U.S.-Cuban relations.)

1960

Feb. 4–13: Soviet Foreign Minister Anastas Mikoyan visited Cuba and signed trade and aid agreements.

Mar. 17: President Eisenhower gave approval for the CIA to begin planning the Bay of Pigs invasion.

May 8: Cuba and the Soviet Union established diplomatic relations.

June 7: U.S. oil companies, at the urging of the Department of State, refused to refine Soviet crude oil at their Cuban refineries. (Later in the same month, Cuba nationalized the refineries.)

July 6: The United States suspended the Cuban sugar quota (effectively cutting off 80 percent of Cuban exports to the United States).

July 10: The Soviet Union agreed to buy Cuban sugar refused by the United States.

Aug. 6: In retaliation for the U.S. suspension of the sugar quota, Cuba nationalized U.S. private investment on the island worth approximately $1 billion.

Aug. 28: The United States imposed an economic embargo against trade with Cuba.

Oct. 14: The Cuban government nationalized all large commercial and industrial enterprises.

1961

Jan. 3: The United States broke relations with Cuba.

Apr. 16: At the funeral of victims of bombing attacks on the eve of the Bay of Pigs invasion, Castro declared that the Cuban revolution was socialist.

Apr. 17–19: A CIA-sponsored invasion force of 1,200 exiles landed at the Bay of Pigs (Playa Girón) and was defeated within seventy-two hours.

Sept. 2: Cuba was the only Latin American state represented at the founding conference of the Non-Aligned Movement.

Dec. 2: Castro declared, "I am a Marxist-Leninist and I shall be one to the end of my life."

1962

Jan. 22–31: The Organization of American States (OAS) launched the Alliance for Progress and suspended Cuba's membership in the organization.

Feb. 4: Castro responded to Cuba's expulsion from the OAS with the Second Declaration of Havana calling upon the people of Latin America to rise up against imperialism and declaring, "The duty of a revolutionary is to make the revolution."

Oct. 16–28: Intermediate-Range Ballistic Missiles provided to Cuba by the Soviet Union triggered the Cuban Missile Crisis, the worst superpower confrontation of the nuclear era. The crisis ended when the Soviet Union agreed, without consulting Cuba, to withdraw the missiles in exchange for a U.S. pledge not to attack the island.

1964

July 26: The OAS adopted mandatory sanctions against Cuba, requiring all members to sever diplomatic and trade relations. (Only Mexico refused to comply.)

1965

Apr. 1: Ernesto "Che" Guevara resigned his Cuban citizenship and left to wage armed struggle in Africa and Latin America.

Oct. 3: The new Communist party of Cuba was inaugurated.

Oct. 10: A boatlift from the port of Camarioca began. (It brought 3,000 Cuban immigrants to the United States in less than one month.)

1966

Jan. 3–15: The first Tricontinental Congress met in Havana. It formed the Organization of Solidarity with the Peoples of Africa, Asia, and Latin America (OSPAAAL) to organize a united front of liberation across three continents. Delegates from twenty-seven Latin American countries created the Latin American Solidarity Organization (OLAS).

Dec. 29: U.S. Air Force pilot Everett Jackson was shot down over Cuba and captured after dropping arms and equipment intended for counter-revolutionaries in Las Villas province.

1967

Apr. 16: Guevara sent a message to the Tricontinental Congress calling for the creation of "two, three, many Vietnams."

May 12: Twelve men, including four Cubans, were intercepted by Venezuelan troops as they landed on a remote Venezuelan beach.

July 31: The first OLAS conference was held in Havana. It declared that guerrilla struggle was the fundamental path to Latin American revolution, though not the only one.

Oct. 9: Guevara was murdered in the Bolivian village of Vallegrande by Bolivian rangers who had been trained by U.S. special forces stationed in Panama. (Within a few days a pair of U.S. Central Intelligence Agency agents identified Guevara's body in Vallegrande.)

1968

Jan. 2: The Cuban government introduced gasoline rationing due to a cutback in deliveries from the Soviet Union. Castro declared that "the dignity of the Revolution demanded that Cubans refrain from begging for additional supplies from the Soviet Union."

Aug. 21: The Soviet Union led the Warsaw Pact in an invasion of Czechoslovakia to buttress the overthrow of the reformist communist regime headed by Alexander Dubcek.

Aug. 23: Castro called the Warsaw Pact invasion a "drastic and painful measure" but a "bitter necessity." He declared that it "saved" socialism in Czechoslovakia and criticized the Czech Communist party for its "bureaucratic methods of leadership."

1969

June 11: Cuba recognized the Provisional Government of South Vietnam.

July 20–27: Seven Soviet naval vessels visited Cuban ports as a show of solidarity between Cuba and the Soviet Union.

Dec.: The first contingent of the Venceremos Brigade, a group of volunteer workers from the United States, arrived in Cuba to work on the sugar harvest.

1970

Sept. 25: The United States warned the Soviet Union to discontinue construction of a nuclear submarine base in Cienfuegos, Cuba. The United States based its demand on the Kennedy-Khrushchev understanding that concluded the 1962 missile crisis, under which the United States promised not to invade Cuba and the Soviet Union promised not to introduce any offensive nuclear weapons in Cuba.

Nov. 12: Chile restored full diplomatic relations with Cuba, one week after the inauguration of Salvador Allende as president.

Nov. 17: The U.S. State Department received assurances from the Soviet Union that no offensive weapons would be introduced into Cuba.

1972

May 3: Castro began a sixty-three-day tour of Africa, Eastern Europe, and the Soviet Union.

July 5: Peru announced the restoration of full diplomatic relations with Cuba.

July 11: Cuba joined the Council for Mutual Economic Assistance (CMEA), the economic organization of the Soviet Union, East European socialist countries, and Mongolia.

Nov. 19: Castro accepted a U.S. proposal to begin formal negotiations over the problem of airline hijackings.

Dec. 8: Barbados, Guyana, Jamaica, and Trinidad and Tobago established diplomatic relations with Cuba.

1973

Feb. 15: The United States and Cuba signed an antihijacking agreement.

May 28: Cuba and Argentina reestablished diplomatic relations.

Sept. 11: Chilean military officers overthrew the democratic government, killed President Allende, and established a military junta to rule the country. (Two days later, Chile broke diplomatic relations with Cuba.)

1974

Jan. 28: Soviet leader Leonid Brezhnev began a week-long visit to Cuba, along with a team of economic specialists.

Apr. 18: The United States agreed to issue export licenses to Argentine subsidiaries of General Motors, Ford, and Chrysler corporations for sales to Cuba.

Aug. 22: Cuba and Panama reestablished diplomatic relations.

Sept.: U.S. Senators Claiborne Pell (D-R.I.) and Jacob Javits (R-N.Y.) visited Cuba, accompanied by a large contingent of journalists. They were the first U.S. officials to visit the island since the break in diplomatic relations.

Nov.: U.S. and Cuban officials secretly met in New York to discuss possible areas for negotiations between the two countries.

Dec. 29: Cuba and Venezuela reestablished diplomatic relations.

1975

Mar. 1: U.S. Secretary of State Henry Kissinger said that the United States was "prepared to move in a new direction" in policy toward Cuba.

July 29: A majority of the OAS, including the United States, voted to lift diplomatic and economic sanctions against Cuba. Each country was free to establish bilateral relations with Cuba. The United States opted to maintain its bilateral embargo.

Aug. 21: The United States announced that it would allow foreign subsidiaries of U.S. companies to sell products in Cuba and that it would no longer penalize other nations for trade with Cuba.

Nov. 5: At the request of the newly inaugurated Angolan government, Cuba sent a battalion of regular troops to help the Angolans repel an invasion launched on October 23 by South African forces.

Dec. 20: President Gerald Ford denounced Soviet and Cuban involvement in Angola and asserted that Cuba's actions would preclude any possibility of reestablishing U.S.-Cuban relations.

1976

Apr. 5: Kissinger asserted that there was no possibility of United States relations with Cuba while Cuba had troops in Africa.

Oct. 6: A bomb on a Cubana Airlines plane exploded after takeoff from Barbados and killed all seventy-three people aboard. (On October 8, in retaliation, Cuba suspended the antihijacking agreement with the United States. Later in the year, Luis Posada Carriles, a Cuban exile and former employee of the U.S. Central Intelligence Agency, was arrested in Venezuela and charged with responsibility for the terrorist act.)

1977

Jan. 25: U.S. United Nations Ambassador Andrew Young declared in an interview that Cuban troops in Angola brought "a certain stability and order" to the southern Africa region.

Mar.: President Jimmy Carter did not renew the ban (renewable every six months) on travel to Cuba by U.S. citizens and lifted the prohibition against the expenditure of money in Cuba by U.S. citizens.

Mar. 16: Castro traveled to the Horn of Africa and attempted to mediate a conflict between Ethiopia and Somalia over possession of the Ogaden region.

Apr. 27: The United States and Cuba signed an accord on fishing rights in boundary waters between the two countries.

May 25: The U.S. State Department stated that it had received reports about the arrival of fifty Cuban military advisers in Ethiopia and warned that Cuban military efforts in that country could "impede the improvement of [U.S.-Cuban] relations."

Oct. 17: Castro visited Jamaica and was warmly received by Prime Minister Michael Manley.

Nov. 5: Somalia expelled all Soviet advisers and broke diplomatic relations with Cuba, citing the presence of Cuban advisers in Ethiopia.

Mid-Dec.: Cuban combat troops began to arrive in Ethiopia.

1978

May 19: The U.S. State Department charged that Cuban troops in Angola were involved in training and encouraging the Katangese rebels in Zaire's Shaba province. (President Carter repeated the charges on May 25, but on June 9 the Senate Foreign Relations Committee found that the evidence for the charges was "inconclusive.")

Sept. 9: Cuban exiles bombed the Cuban Mission to the United Nations in New York.

Oct. 21: In an attempt at reconciliation with the Cuban-American community, Cuba released forty-six prisoners and ex-prisoners who then flew to the United States. (Later in the year the Committee of 75 was formed to act as a representative of Cubans living abroad.)

1979

Jan. 1: Cuban-Americans were permitted to visit their families in Cuba. (More than 100,000 did this during 1979.)

Mar. 13: The dictatorship of Eric Gairy in Grenada was overthrown in a bloodless coup by the broad-based New Jewel Movement, headed by Maurice Bishop, who became prime minister.

Apr. 14: Grenada established diplomatic relations with Cuba. (Subsequently the two countries developed close economic and political ties.)

July 19: A broad coalition led by the Sandinista National Liberation Front overthrew the dictatorship of Anastasio Somoza in Nicaragua.

July 26: The annual celebration to commemorate the 1953 attack on the Moncada barracks was dedicated to the Nicaragua revolution. Three members of the new Nicaraguan government attended the ceremonies.

Aug. 30: As delegates to the sixth summit of the Non-Aligned Movement gathered in Havana, the United States charged that a new 3,000-troop Soviet combat brigade had been discovered in Cuba. Cuba and the Soviet Union asserted (and later congressional hearings confirmed) that the brigade was a training group that had been stationed in Cuba since 1962.

Sept. 3–9: The sixth summit of the Non-Aligned Movement met in Havana. Castro was elected chair of the movement and served until 1982.

Oct. 1: President Carter announced several responses to the alleged Soviet combat brigade in Cuba, including the establishment of a U.S. military headquarters in Key West, Florida, and expanded military maneuvers in the Caribbean and out of Guantanamo Naval Base.

Nov. 6: The first contingent of Cuban teachers left for Nicaragua.

1980

Jan. 11: President Fidel Castro assumed responsibility in the Communist Party Central Committee for the ministries of Defense, Interior, Public Health, and Culture.

Mar. 12: Cubans began work in Grenada on a new international airport, which became an object of concern for the United States. (At about this time, Cuba also sent medical teams and technical personnel to support the New Jewel Movement government in Grenada.)

Apr. 1: Twelve people seeking asylum used a minibus to crash through the gates of the Peruvian Embassy in Havana. (Within the same week, the Cuban government removed guards from the embassy, and Peru announced that its embassy grounds would be open for anyone who wished to enter, an offer that 7,000 people accepted.)

Apr. 21: Cuba announced that anyone wishing to leave the country could be picked up at the port of Mariel. (By September 26, when the port was closed, 120,000 had left the country, most going to the United States. Approximately 1 percent were people released from prisons and mental institutions.)

May 2: After a fight broke out between demonstrators and former prisoners waiting for visas to be processed, 389 former political prisoners took refuge in the U.S. Interests Section in Havana.

Oct. 31: Newly elected Jamaican Prime Minister Edward Seaga asked Cuba to withdraw its ambassador, Ulises Estrada, in a first step toward a break in relations.

Dec. 17–20: The Second Congress of Cuban Communist Party ratified a five-year plan that projected a 5 percent growth rate and called for increased efficiency. The main report of the congress attributed the failure to achieve the 6 percent rate anticipated in 1975 to a dramatic increase in interest rates on foreign capital and diseases that affected sugar and tobacco crops.

1981

Jan. 20: The Territorial Troop Militia was launched at a ceremony in Granma province. (By 1985 it had 1.5 million members, composed of people who were in neither the regular nor reserve forces.)

Feb. 18: U.S. Secretary of State Alexander Haig told NATO representatives that the United States had "to deal with the immediate source of the problem [in El Salvador]—and that is Cuba."

Feb. 20: Mexico agreed to purchase 100,000 tons of Cuban sugar, three days after U.S. General Vernon Walters had presented President Jose Lopez Portillo with "evidence" of Cuban support for the guerrillas in El Salvador.

Feb. 22: Edwin Meese, counsel to the president, declared that he would not "rule out anything," in response to a question about whether the United States would consider a blockade to stop alleged arms shipments from Cuba to El Salvador.

Mar. 23: Colombia suspended diplomatic relations with Cuba, charging that Cuba had trained and armed several dozen M-19 guerrillas. Cuba categorically denied the charge.

Oct. 29: Jamaica broke relations with Cuba and expelled Cubans working there.

Oct. 30: The U.S. Navy began four weeks of exercises in the Caribbean. (Pentagon officials said on November 6 that the maneuvers were expected to send a message to Cuba.)

Oct. 31: Cuba mobilized its reserves and went on full alert in preparation for an anticipated U.S. invasion.

Nov. 5: Secretary of State Haig confirmed a report in the *New York Times* that disclosed that he had been "pressing the Defense Department to develop contingency options for action against Nicaragua and Cuba."

Nov. 23: Cuban Vice President Carlos Rafael Rodriguez met secretly with Secretary Haig in Mexico. No agreements were reached.

Nov. 24: President Lopez Portillo warned Secretary Haig that military action against Cuba would be a "great historical error."

1982

Feb. 24: At the General Assembly of the Organization of American States, President Reagan declared that the 1981 Cuban military buildup and the introduction of MIG-23/Flogger aircraft into the Cuban arsenal threatened the "security of our neighbors in this region." He warned that "we will do whatever is prudent and necessary to ensure the peace and security of the Caribbean area."

Apr. 10: Following Cuban offers of aid to Argentina in the Malvinas/Falklands conflict, the Cuban ambassador to Argentina returned to Buenos Aires after a long absence. (Two days later Argentina sent its ambassador back to Cuba, and on June 3 the two countries signed a new trade agreement.)

Apr. 19: The U.S. Treasury Department—in a move proclaimed to tighten the embargo against Cuba—announced the reimposition of restrictions on travel to Cuba. (Beginning May 15, only four categories of people were permitted to spend money in Cuba—without a special license—in relation to their travel there: U.S. government officials, scholars, journalists, and Cuban exiles visiting their families.)

Apr. 29: The U.S. Navy launched Operation Ocean Venture 82 (a three-week Caribbean maneuver that involved 45,000 troops, 350 airplanes, and 60 ships. It included a noncombatant evacuation exercise of Guantanamo Naval Base.)

June 16: Vice President Rodriguez told the UN that Cuba had almost doubled its military strength since 1981, in response to the aggressiveness of the Reagan administration.

1983

Jan. 10: The U.S. State Department reported that Cuba received 50 MIG-23 aircraft and 140 SAM-3 missiles in 1982.

Jan. 11: Cuba and Bolivia reestablished diplomatic relations.

Mar. 1: Cuba signed an agreement with thirteen creditor nations to reschedule its $810 million foreign debt due between September 1, 1982, and December 31, 1983.

July 24: President Castro, in a letter to the Contadora Group (Mexico, Panama, Colombia, and Venezuela), declared that Cuba would cooperate with any negotiated solution toward peace. (Four days later, he asserted that Cuba would be willing to agree to the withdrawal of military advisers in Nicaragua and a ban on arms transfers in the region if "all parties involved" also complied with restrictions on advisers and arms.)

Oct. 19: Grenadian Prime Minister Maurice Bishop was assassinated in the middle of civil strife over his deposition by a rival New Jewel Movement faction. Bishop had had close personal ties with President Castro.

Oct. 22: Cuba denied a request from Grenada to assist it militarily in the face of an impending U.S. attack.

Oct. 25: The United States invaded Grenada with 8,800 troops, occupied the island, and established a provisional government. (Of the 784 Cubans on the island, 636 were construction workers and 43 were military personnel. The United States captured 642 Cubans, killed 24, and wounded 57.)

1984

Mar. 19: Cuba and Angola outlined conditions under which Cuba would withdraw its troops, including removal of all South African forces from Namibia and implementation of UN Security Council Resolution 435.

Apr. 20: Commencement of U.S. war games—Ocean Venture 84 (which included a mock evacuation from Guantanamo Naval Base).

May 14: The U.S. Department of Defense reported that it would spend $43 million to refurbish Guantanamo Naval Base.

June 28: The U.S. Supreme Court ruled that the Treasury Department could impose on U.S. citizens restrictions that had the effect of banning travel to Cuba.

June 29: Presidential candidate Jesse Jackson left Cuba after a series of meetings that resulted in the release of twenty-six prisoners, further openings for the church in Cuba, and the agreement by Cuba to open talks on immigration issues with the United States.

Dec. 14: The United States and Cuba reached agreement on an immigration program under which Cuba would repatriate 2,746 "excludables" who had arrived during the Mariel exodus, and the United States would permit the immigration of 20,000 Cubans annually.

1985

Jan. 24: Five U.S. Catholic church leaders met with President Castro and high Cuban officials. This followed the opening earlier in the month of the Office of Religious Affairs, which signaled warmer relations between the Cuban government and church. José Felipe Carneado, a member of the Communist Party Central Committee, was selected to head the Office.

Mar. 13: President Castro declined to attend the funeral of Soviet Communist Party Chairman Konstantin Chernenko, indicating strains between the Soviet Union and Cuba.

May 19: The United States initiated propaganda broadcasts to Cuba over Radio Marti. In response, Cuba suspended the five-month old immigration and repatriation agreement with the United States.

Aug. 3: A five-day conference in Havana on foreign debt concluded with a call for a basic restructuring of the relationship between debtor and creditor nations. Attending the conference were 1,200 delegates from 37 hemispheric countries.

Oct. 4: President Reagan issued a proclamation that banned travel to the United States by Cuban government or Communist party officials or their representatives, which effectively barred most students, scholars, and artists as well as officials.

Oct. 17: Uruguay renewed diplomatic relations with Cuba.

1986

Feb. 7: The Third Congress of the Cuban Communist Party ratified proposals to coordinate Cuba's economic plans more closely with the Council for Mutual Economic Assistance, to improve economic efficiency, to increase representation in the party hierarchy and in the party itself by women, workers, and other underrepresented sectors, and to support Nicaragua.

Feb. 17: The Cuban Catholic church hosted an international conference about the church in Cuba, attended by bishops from most Latin American countries and the United States and a Vatican representative.

Apr. 11: The Soviet Union agreed to a five-year, $3 billion program of aid and economic credit for Cuba.

June 25: Brazil reestablished diplomatic relations with Cuba.

July 8: Cuban and U.S. officials met in Mexico to discuss a resumption of the immigration agreement and the possible broadcast to the United States of a Cuban radio station. The meeting ended in stalemate.

1987

Mar. 11: The United Nations Human Rights Commission voted down a U.S. resolution that harshly criticized Cuba for alleged human rights violations. Only one of the eight Latin American nations on the commission voted with the United States.

May 28: General Rafael del Pino, an official in the Cuban Air Force, defected to the United States. (In interviews throughout the summer and fall on Radio Marti, he charged that there were serious morale problems in the Cuban military and that there were thousands of Cuban casualties in Angola.)

June 6: Major Florentino Aspillaga Lombard, a Cuban intelligence officer in Czechoslovakia, defected and subsequently came to the United States. (His interviews on Radio Marti in the fall generated turmoil in the Miami Cuban community because of false charges against several people and organizations that they were part of a Cuban espionage network.)

July 6: Cuban television began a seven-part documentary with dramatic on-the-scene footage that detailed espionage activities by U.S. officials stationed in the U.S. Interests Section (diplomatic mission) in Havana. Four of the officials allegedly involved in spying worked at the interests section when the program was aired.

July 15: In retaliation for the Cuban television series, the United States expelled two Cuban diplomats stationed at the Cuban Interests Section in Washington.

Aug. 10: The U.S. State Department announced that it was reviewing a new Angolan proposal about the Cuban military presence there. (This followed talks between President Castro and Angolan President Eduardo dos Santos.)

Aug. 13: President Castro endorsed the Central American (Arias) peace plan approved by the leaders of the five affected countries on August 7 in Guatamala. Also on August 13, following a two-day meeting in Havana with Nicaraguan President Daniel Ortega, the Cuban leader said that Cuba would be willing to abide by agreements that might call for the removal of all foreign military advisers from Central America.

Oct. 19: In a decision with potential impact on the implementation of a 1985 presidential proclamation, the U.S. Supreme Court upheld a ruling by a federal Court of Appeals that barred the State Department from denying a visa to a person solely on the basis of membership in a Communist party.

Nov. 20: The United States and Cuba restored the immigration agreement that Cuba had cancelled in 1985.

Suggested Readings

General Information About Cuba

Philip Brenner, William LeoGrande, Donna Rich, and Daniel Siegel, eds. *The Cuba Reader.* New York: Grove Press, forthcoming.

Cuba Update. Published by the Center for Cuban Studies, 124 West 23rd Street, New York, New York 10011.

Juan M. del Aguila. *Cuba: Dilemmas of a Revolution.* Boulder, Colo.: Westview Press, 1984.

Jorge I. Dominguez. *Cuba: Order and Revolution.* Cambridge: Harvard University Press, 1978.

Sandor Halebsky and John M. Kirk, eds. *Cuba: Twenty-Five Years of Revolution, 1959–1984.* New York: Praeger, 1985.

Herbert L. Matthews. *Revolution in Cuba.* New York: Scribner's, 1975.

James D. Rudolph, ed. *Cuba: A Country Study.* U.S. Army Foreign Area Studies Handbook Series. Washington, D.C.: Government Printing Office, 1987.

Hugh S. Thomas, Georges A. Fauriol, and Juan Carlos Weiss, eds. *The Cuban Revolution: 25 Years Later.* Boulder, Colo.: Westview Press, 1984.

Cuban History

Luis E. Aguilar. *Cuba 1933: Prologue to Revolution.* New York: Norton, 1974.

Jules Robert Benjamin. *The United States and Cuba: Hegemony and Dependent Development, 1900–1934.* Pittsburgh: University of Pittsburgh Press, 1977.

Robin Blackburn. "Prologue to the Cuban Revolution," *New Left Review* (London), October 1963.

Philip S. Foner. *A History of Cuba and Its Relations With the U.S.* 2 vols. New York: International Publishing Co., 1962, 1963.

Jose Marti. *Obras Completas.* Havana: Editorial Nacional de Cuba, 1963.

James O'Connor. *The Origins of Socialism in Cuba.* Ithaca: Cornell University Press, 1970.

Louis A. Perez, Jr. *Cuba Under the Platt Amendment, 1902–1934.* Pittsburgh: University of Pittsburgh Press, 1986.

Julio Le Riverend, *Economic History of Cuba.* Havana: Ensayo Book Institute, 1967.

Robert F. Smith. *The United States and Cuba: Business and Diplomacy, 1917–1960.* New Haven: College and University Press, 1960.

Hugh Thomas. *Cuba, or The Pursuit of Freedom.* London: Eyre & Spottiswoode, 1971. A shorter version, with an epilogue, is available in paperback: *The Cuban Revolution.* New York: Harper and Row, 1977.

Aspects of Contemporary Cuba

Medea Benjamin, Joseph Collins, and Michael Scott. *No Free Lunch: Food and Revolution in Cuba Today.* San Francisco: Institute for Food and Development Policy, 1984.

Frei Betto. *Fidel and Religion.* New York: Simon and Schuster, 1987.

Claes Brundenius. *Revolutionary Cuba: The Challenge of Economic Growth with Equity.* Boulder, Colo.: Westview Press, 1984.

Richard Fagen. *The Transformation of Political Culture in Cuba.* Stanford: Stanford University Press, 1969.

Norberto Fuentes. *Nos Impusieron La Violencia.* Havana: Editorial Letras Cubanas, 1986.

Edward Gonzalez. *Cuba Under Castro: The Limits of Charisma.* Boston: Houghton Mifflin, 1974.

Jonathan Kozol. *Children of the Revolution.* New York: Delacorte, 1978.

Frank Mankiewicz and Kirby Jones. *With Fidel: A Portrait of Castro and Cuba.* New York: Ballantine, 1975.

Seymour Menton. *Prose Fiction of the Cuban Revolution.* Austin: University of Texas Press, 1975.

Carmelo Mesa-Lago. *The Economy of Socialist Cuba: A Two-Decade Appraisal.* Albuquerque: University of New Mexico Press, 1981.

Carlos Rafael Rodriguez. *Letra Con Filo.* 2 vols. Havana: Editorial de Ciencias Sociales, 1983.

Bertram Silverman, ed. *Man and Socialism in Cuba: The Great Debate.* New York: Atheneum, 1971.

Tad Szulc. *Fidel: A Critical Portrait.* New York: Morrow, 1986.

Andrew Zimbalist. *Cuba's Socialist Economy Toward the 1990s.* Boulder, Colo.: Lynne Rienner Publishers, 1987.

Cuban Foreign Policy

Cole Blasier and Carmelo Mesa-Lago, eds. *Cuba in the World.* Pittsburgh: University of Pittsburgh Press, 1979.

Fidel Castro. *The World Economic and Social Crisis.* Havana: Publishing Office of the Council of State, 1983.

Jorge I. Dominguez. "Cuban Foreign Policy." *Foreign Affairs,* Fall 1978.

H. Michael Erisman. *Cuba's International Relations: The Anatomy of a Nationalistic Foreign Policy.* Boulder, Colo.: Westview Press, 1985.

Pamela S. Falk. *Cuban Foreign Policy.* Lexington, Mass.: D. C. Heath, 1986.

Jane Franklin. *Cuban Foreign Relations: A Chronology, 1959–1982.* New York: Center for Cuban Studies, 1984.

William M. LeoGrande. *Cuba's Policy in Africa, 1959–1980.* Policy Papers in International Affairs, no. 13. Institute of International Studies. Berkeley: University of California, 1980.

Barry B. Levine, ed. *The New Cuban Presence in the Caribbean.* Boulder, Colo.: Westview Press, 1983.

Carla Anne Robbins. *The Cuban Threat.* New York: McGraw-Hill, 1983.

U.S.-Cuban Relations

Graham Allison. *Essence of Decision.* Boston: Little, Brown, 1971.

Philip Bonsal. *Cuba, Castro and the United States.* Pittsburgh: University of Pittsburgh Press, 1971.

Philip Brenner. *The Limits and Possibilities of Congress.* New York: St. Martin's Press, 1983.

Raymond L. Garthoff. *Intelligence Assessment and Policymaking: A Decision Point in the Kennedy Administration.* Washington, D.C.: Brookings Institution, 1984.

Robert F. Kennedy. *Thirteen Days: A Memoir of the Cuban Missile Crisis.* New York: New American Library, 1969.

William M. LeoGrande. "Cuba." In *Confronting Revolution: Security Through Diplomacy in Central America,* ed. Morris J. Blachman, William M. LeoGrande, Kenneth Sharpe. New York: Pantheon, 1986.

Wayne S. Smith. *The Closest of Enemies: A Personal and Diplomatic Account of U.S.-Cuban Relations Since 1957.* New York: Norton, 1987.

Peter Wyden. *Bay of Pigs: The Untold Story.* New York: Simon and Schuster, 1979.

Index